Olive Oil

EAT BETTER,
LIVE LONGER

134 Recipes with olive oil
20 Recipes with olives

Myrsini Lambraki

TITLE: Olive Oil. Eat better, live longer
AUTHOR: Myrsini Lambraki
COPYRIGHT: Myrsini Lambraki
                 Raftopoulou Sr. 31,
                 71305 Heraklion, Crete
TEL.& FAX: +30-81-210.052 & 346.554
MOBILE PHONE: 0945. 468190
E-MAIL: mirsini@her.forthnet.gr - web site://users.forthnet.gr/her/mi
FIRST EDITION: March 1999
ISBN: 960-91513-0-2
TRANSLATION (TEXT): Maria Teresa Xylouri
TRANSLATION (RECIPES): Vicky Smyrli, Aggela Shinaraki
PHOTOGRAPHS: Panagiotis Beltzinitis, Myrsini Lambraki
COVER PHOTOGRAPHS: Douwe Hoogstins
LAYOUT: MKS Metaxaraki Advertising

TABLE OF
Contents

52 RECIPES

143 OLIVES, THE MOST IMPORTANT FOOD

146 RECIPES WITH OLIVES

WHAT IS OLIVE OIL?

1 IDENTITY OF THE PRECIOUS TREE

Cultivated olive trees belong to the botanical group Sativa which, together with oleaster, a cousin of the same plant, are a sub-species of the Olea europaea. The Mediterranean, with its hot dry summers and cool winters with soft rains, is the ideal habitat of this tree.

Olive trees are not particularly demanding and can be grown on poor stony ground, unsuitable for other crops. An evergreen, it takes the olive tree 5 to 8 years to produce its first fruit, but the tree has an extremely long and productive life: up to 600 years, sometimes more. There are over 75 varieties of olives.

2 ETYMOLOGY

The word "olive" has European and Asian roots that denote its origin. It can be traced as far back as the Cretan word "elaiwa" and the Semitic word "ulu", becoming "oleum" in Latin.

On the other hand the Spanish word for oil, "aceite", has a totally different origin and comes from the word "zait" and "zaitum" in Arabic.

Man's first contact with the olive tree... the shiny green fruit and the slivery leaves shimering in the Mediterran e an sun... When did the miracle occur?

The life giving juice

3 OLIVE OIL: THE JUICE OF THE OLIVES

Olive oil is the oil obtained from the fruit of the olive tree in a mechanical manner: the liquid is pressed out of the fruit of the olive tree and then separated from the mass of the squashed fruit by centrifugal force or else by precipitation.

One wonders when it was that Man had his first taste of the olive, the sweet unknown taste filling his mouth after that first bite... an earthy primordial life giving taste, very similar to that of wheat and barley...

4 FIRST APPEARANCE OF THE OLIVE TREE IN THE MEDITTERANEAN

There is no way of knowing when the olive tree first made its appearance. It is as if this tree wanted to keep its secret forever, making us believe it is as old as the world, as sacred as the oldest mysteries, a precious and unique gift from the gods to mankind. It is impossible to imagine Greece without the tree that gives it life, the olive tree. Beyond historical and archaeological facts, only mythology has the power to explain its origins...

5 THE MYTHS

According to Ionian mythology, the father of the gods promised the land of Attica to the god or goddess who would give it the most original and useful gift. Athena, the goddess of Wisdom, won the land from Poseidon, by offering an olive tree, the symbol of welfare and peace. This is why the city was called after the goddess and the sacred olive tree was carefully tended on the rock of the Acropolis. However, Cretan mythology has it that the goddess Athena was born in Crete at the mouth of the river Tritonas and made a gift of the sacred tree to the inhabitants of the island. According to a third myth, Daktylos Hercules travelling in a Minoan ship, reached the Peloponnese and from there the olive tree he carried with him spread to the whole of Greece.

HISTORICAL BACKGROUND

Although the homeland of the olive tree is not exactly known, it is generally accepted that this tree originated in Syria and other eastern Mediterranean countries. From there, it expanded to all the Mediterranean basin. According to a 12th century BC Egyptian papyrus, the Pharaoh Ramesses III made an offering of the tree to Ra, the god of sun. We find other significant traces of the olive tree in the Bible:Noah, in Genesis, knows that the waters of the flood have subsided when a dove brings him a small olive branch to the Ark; Homer maintains that the olive tree has been thriving in Greece for over 10.000 years and one of Solon's laws sentenced to death anyone found guilty of uprooting or destroying an olive tree.

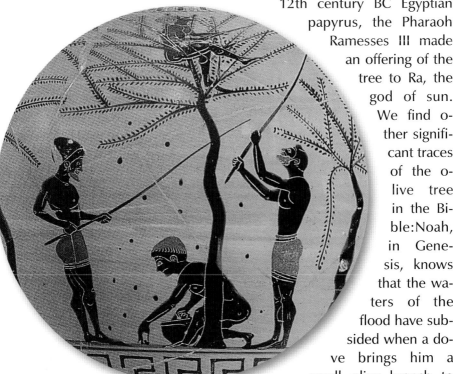

Olive harvest on a 530 BC aphora from Attica.

CRETE, THE MOST IMPORTANT LANDMARK IN THE HISTORY OF THE OLIVE TREE

Olive trees are thought to have been first cultivated during the Early Bronze Age, in the third millennium BC.

The island of Crete may well have been the most decisive landmark in the development of this culture and there is little doubt that the small and lithe Minoans were the ones to take over the culture of the olive tree from other eastern Mediterranean peoples. It is here, where the climate is mild and the land fertile, where one of the most important civilizations in the world was developing, that the olive tree found its ideal home. Here it blossomed, giving its oil in plenty, revered and honoured as no other tree. The unique and rich archaeological finds underline the importance that the olive tree had

Beautiful perennial olive trees cover the island, their robustness a living proof of their continual presence.

*A Linear B inscription representing
an olive tee and olive oil.*

THE SYMBOL

The sacred olive tree, blessed by ancient and modern gods alike, of which we find references in Homer, in ancient Egyptian papyri, in the Old and the New Testaments and the Coran, is a symbol of knowledge, wisdom, abundance, peace, strength, beauty and health -a living myth among the Greeks, revered in ancient and in modern times...

in every day life, but also in Minoan rituals. The vast majority of these finds are exhibited in local museums across the island; they include stone olive presses, storing jars for the oil, lamps, and various representations of the tree or of olive branches on all sorts of vessels, including sarcophagi. It is noteworthy how the olive tree is often represented in religious rituals.

The most spectacular archaeological find was found at the Minoan Palace at Zakros: a conical cup full of olives...

*A tetradrachm coin representing
an owl and an olive branch,
symbols of the goddes Athena.*

*Conical clay vase dated to the 16th century BC found
at the Palace of Zakros full of olives (Heraklion Museum).*

THE USES OF OLIVE OIL IN ANTIQUITY

Olive oil in antiquity was used, plain or mixed with aromatic herbs, flowers or spices, in the beauty care of body and hair. The oil gave an aesthetic shine to the athletes bodies, and at the same time gave extra protection to their muscles. Skin diseases were treated with poultices and unguents prepared

running contest was given about two and a half tons of the very best olive oil which he was allowed to sell and export, an exclusive right awarded to Olympic winners).

In Antiquity men, women and even athletes used perfumed olive oil as a cosmetic.

with olive oil.

Olive oil was also used in cooking -to add taste to the different types of food-, in lighting houses and temples, in offerings to the gods and the dead, as prizes in contests (the winners at the Olympic Games received a large number of olive oil jars and the winner of the

THE USES OF OLIVE OIL NOWADAYS

Greeks consume about 22 kilograms of olive oil a year per head; no other fat substance is used in Greek kitchens, whether at home or in the tavernas and restaurants.

Byzantine miniature from 11th century. Bottom. Greek coins with olive branches

CRETE THE ISLAND OF THE OLIVE TREE

THIRTY MILLION OLIVE TREES

The island of Crete, the largest in Greece, has a total area of 8.336 square km. of which 30% are plains, 27% low mountains and about 50% high mountains. The cultivated land covers about 37% of the total, that is 360.000 hectares, of which 55% are taken by olive trees.

Foreigners visiting Crete are often astonished when they realize to what an extent the olive tree is cultivated in this little corner of the south-eastern Mediterranean. The variety is striking: olive trees in Crete grow close to the towns and in the towns, on the fertile plains, on the sunny hills and on the high mountains; some are small, others large, others so old that their trunks stand out among the orange groves and the endless vineyards.

CLIMATE, SOIL AND MEN: THE PERFECT BALANCE

Fertile plains and high mountains are the two most striking elements in the Cretan landscape. Along the mountain chains, thousands of olive trees grow on rather poor soil; the olive tree, as we said before, is not demanding, and willingly brings forth its fruit on all soils. The mild winters with soft rains and long periods of sunshine provide perfect conditions for optimal results. The winds from the sea are rarely harsh, and in spring and summer -hot but not burning hot- the olive trees stretch out their branches and drink in the life-giving rays of the sun. The olives "swell" in the autumn softness, full of oil, and Cretans love their olive trees as if they were members of the family. As in ancient times, the olive tree forms part of their lives, playing an important role not just in their diet, but in their civilization and in their art.

The deeply rooted ties between Cretans and olive tree: a symbol of life, it cures body and soul it forms part of their every day life and their daily diet. It is considered a member of the family.

PRODUCTION AND CONSUMPTION OF OLIVES AND OLIVE OIL IN CRETE

Olive groves in Crete occupy some 160.000 hectares and around 30 million trees are cultivated by 95.000 families.

The increase in olive oil production in Crete in the past 40 years has been spectacular, duplicating twice over. The quality has also improved significantly and, in the last 15 years, practically all Cretan oil (90%) is of extra virgin quality with an acidity level of less than 1 degree. Olive oil consumption is very high on the island, reaching close to 30 kg per head - the highest consumption of olive oil per capita in the world.

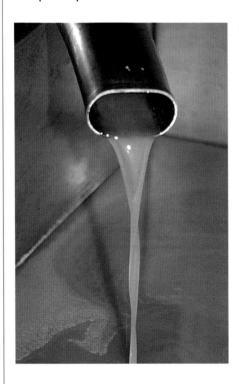

Novadays the olive oil produced on the islands is all of the finest quality, with unique attributes and a distinctive aroma.

EXPORTATIONS

Scandinavian countries, England, Austria, Germany and North America are the main countries importing large amounts of bottled Cretan first-rate olive oil. A large quantity of Cretan and in general Greek unbottled olive oil is also bought by the Italians to improve the quality and fragrance of their own oil.

VARIETY OF OLIVE TREES

There are basically three different categories of olive trees in Crete, each kind producing large amounts of both olive oil and edible olives.

a) The Olea Europea variety, Mastoides (Koronaiki): this is a very important variety not just in Crete but all over Greece. In spite of its small olives, it is resistant and can be grown up to an altitude of 500 metres; it bears fruit regularly, each tree yielding an average of 150 kg. This variety is found in the following regions in Crete: Chania, Heraklion, Lassithi and Sitia. It produces an oil of excellent quality and fragrance.

b) The Olea Europea variety, Media oblonga (Throumbolia-Chontrolia): this variety is the classical one in Crete, and although part of the traditional culture has been replaced nowadays with the Koronaiki variety (see above), it continues to be much grown across the island. It can be grown at an altitude of 700 metres and gives a rich, sweet oil on condition that the olives are picked as soon as they fall from

Branches with ripe Hontrolies - throumpes

the tree and immediately pressed.
c) The Olea Europea variety,
Mamilaris (Tsounati): this is the
kind most resistant to climatic
extremities. It is grown mainly in
the area of Chania and gives first
rate olive oil.

*Bread, olive oil and coarse salt, or else,
olive oil cinnemon and sugar used to
be the children's most beloved snack.*

OLIVE OIL IN CRETAN DIET

For centuries Europeans and
Americans have been using animal
fat for cooking, mainly butter and
pork fat; Cretans have never
known these fats and have
exclusively used olive oil
in their kitchens.
When Robert Pa-
shley, an Eng-
lish traveller
came to Cre-
te in the first
half of the
19th century,
he was astoni-
shed at the consu-
mption of olive oil: "I
am told here, as in
every other place
where I have made
enquiries, respecting
the consumption of
oil by each Cretan
family, that it may be
estimated at 4 okes
(a little over 5 kilo-
grams) a week, at least.

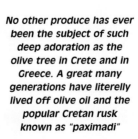

*No other produce has ever
been the subject of such
deep adoration as the
olive tree in Crete and in
Greece. A great many
generations have literelly
lived off olive oil and the
popular Cretan rusk
known as "paximadi"*

A mother will hardly give bread to
her children without pouring them
out some oil into a dish, that
they may moisten the
staff of life, and
render it more
savory, before
eating it. Oil
is used on all
kinds of vege-
tables, as well
as in preparing
every sort of meat
and fish: in short it
enters into every dish
in Crete, and though
all Greeks use a good
deal of it, there is a
much greater general
consumption of it in
this island than else-
where."

SCIENTIFIC VERIFICATION

A little more than a century later the American Rockfeller Institute carried out a research between 1948 and 1957 among the inhabitants of Crete, declaring in its report: "Cretan diet consists mainly of vegetarian products such as cereals, vegetables, fruit and olive oil... Olives and oil play an important part in the resistance of a Cretan constitution. A foreigner might find that Cretan food actually swims in oil: the consumption of olive oil is a distinctive attribute of the Cretan diet.".

Olive oil generously enriches all Cretan food.

OLIVE OIL IN CRETAN COOKING

The deeply rooted and continuous relation of Cretans with olive oil goes far back in Antiquity. For centuries, olive oil has been curing both body and soul and is an indispensable element of the daily diet. Oil is generously poured on all casserole food, on boiled food, roasts, fried food and even in the delicious sweetmeats and pastries. Raw, it is used for salad dressings and bread and rusks are often soaked in its delicious and lovely glossiness .

*Cretan cooking
with olive oil
gives off
a wonderful smell,
the fresh
vegetabless retain
all their freshness
and the
salads shine
in the
translucent
gold color
of the oil...*

Old traditional Greek olive press with stone grinder being worked by a donkey.

OLIVE OIL A LIFE INCURANCE

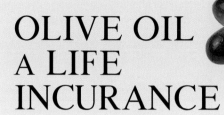

COMPOSITION OF OLIVE OIL

Vitamin E (3-30 mg)
Provitamin A (carotene)
Monounsaturated fatty acids
(oleic) 56-83%
Polyunsaturated unfatty acid
(Linoleic) 3.5-20%
Polyunsaturated fatty acid
(Linolenic) 0-1.5%
Saturated fatty acids 8-23.5%
9 calories per gram

OLIVE OIL, THE HEALTHIEST OF ALL FATS

Fat used in food finds a healthy substitute in olive oil which is 77% monounsaturated fat and naturally cholesterol-free. Olive oil contains no salt, and one tablespoon provides 8%RDA for vitamin E. Olive oil is gluten-free. Gluten is found in wheat and rye, and to a lesser degree, in barley and oats, but not in 100% pure olive oil.

THE STRONGEST HEARTS IN THE WORLD ARE THE CRETAN HEARTS

The Cretan diet has, over the last few years, been under scientific and medical study, and dietetics and statistics have proved that it ensures good health and longevity. The consumption of olive oil is the main reason for the low number of cardiac disorders among the inhabitants of the island.

OLIVE OIL, CHOLESTEROL AND CORONARY DISEASE

Olive oil decreases unwanted cholesterol and limits arteriosclerosis, which is one of the main causes of death in industrial areas where butter and pork fat are used in cooking. Its monounsaturated oleic acid is as effective as its polyunsaturated fatty acids in decreasing the total amount of cholesterol in the blood and it has a positive effect on the HDL, the

Olive oil has been for centuries the main source of good health and longevity among Cretans.

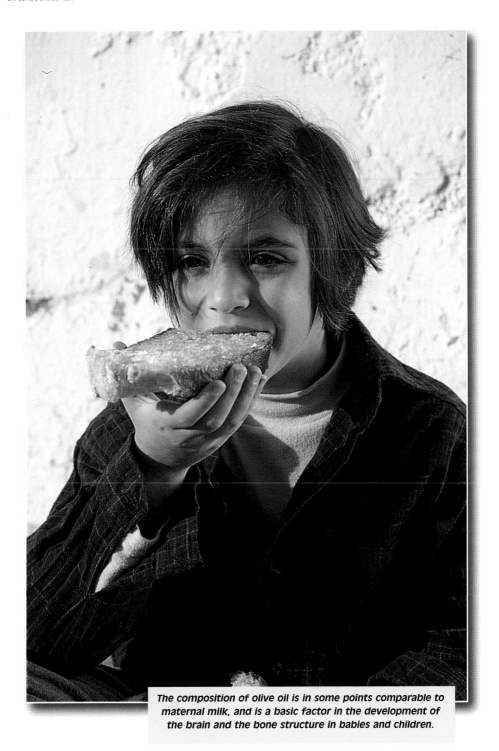

The composition of olive oil is in some points comparable to maternal milk, and is a basic factor in the development of the brain and the bone structure in babies and children.

protective factor against coronary disease.

OLIVE OIL AND CALORIES

Many people wonder whether olive oil has more calories than other cooking oils. The answer is: NO. Olive oil has 120 calories per tablespoon. Furthermore, its rich fragrance allows one to use less quantity of olive oil than one would of other less rich oils, thereby reducing the intake of calories even more.

OLIVE OIL AND GOOD HEALTH

- Olive oil has a beneficial effect on peptic ulcers and on indigestion

- It is easily absorbed by the intestine and functions as a mild purgative

- Olive oil is rich in monounsaturated fatty acids which are precious in the composition of lipids, which in turn are essential to the reproduction of human cells, the basic element of all human organism

- Vitamin E and pro-vitamin A contained in olive oil protect the skin from harmful sun rays and burns

- Olive oil contributes to the development of the bones, especially in children and adolescents

- The composition of olive oil resembles that of maternal milk and is most efficient in the development of the central nervous system in babies and children

- Olive oil, due to the antioxidant elements in it contains, protects the brain and keeps it alert in old age

- There are less cases of some types of cancer (e.g., cancer of the breast and cancer of the ovaries) in the Mediterranean basin, due to the consumption of olive oil

- Olive oil plays a significant role in counteracting diabetic atrophy

- Rich in tokopheroles, it contains many antioxidant elements.

THE OLIVE TREE AND OLIVE OIL MUSEUM IN KAPSALIANA

The small village Kapsaliana is situated on the road from Rethymno towards the historical monastery of Arkadi.
The building was constructed by the Venetians during the 16th century and belonged to the monastery of Arkadi.
It was renovated in the 17th century by the monk of Filareto. The production of olive oil for the monastery led to the foundation and exisence of the village. Even

today the area constitutes one of the oldest and most importand olive groves in Crete.

The olive oil millstone of the monastery, the wooden press and unique stone troughs, in addition to the rare stone carving can be found in the center of the village. The wooden door frames are full

A rare kind: this "blond" olive is found at the entrance of the museum.

of notes made by the monks, detailing the quantity of olives gathered at the end of the 19th century.

The olive millstone and the press were in use for more than 300 years and breathed life into the village.

The village was deserted following the second world war and currently the architect Miron Tupogiannis, is in the process of rebuilding the village. His aim is to establish an olive tree and olive museum. Various activities will take place including periodical exhibitions, cultural exchanges, lectures, gastronomical events, handicrafts. Moreover a guest house will be available.

Carved stone basin for collecing olive oil. Above, an "iconostasis" where the monks had an oil lamp burning night and day, blessing the precious liquid.

OLIVE OIL PRODUCTION IN GREECE

Map of the oil production in Greece.

The most precious product in Greece is undoubtedly olive oil. Over 350.000 families (half of them in the Peloponnese and in Crete) live from their oil produce. Olive oil covers 80% of the fat and oil consumption. There are 2.800 olive oil presses in Greece and 220 bottling companies. 30% of the Greek olive oil is produced in Crete, 26% in the Peloponnese, 10% in Lesbos and another 10% in the Ionian islands. Mainland Greece, Evia and Chalkidiki produce very good quality oil, as do the Cycladic and Sporadic islands though in a lesser quantity.

THE PELOPONNESE

One of the principal regions for the production of olive oil is the Peloponnese where the systematic culture of the olive tree began as far back as the 16th century. In fact between the 16th

Large olives of the Chalkidiki area.

Kalamata, Mani and Olympia. Kalamata and all the surrounding region also produce the world famous "Kalamata" olives, both green and black, large, fleshy and spicy.

HOW IS OLIVE OIL PRODUCED

THE HARVEST

and the 19th centuries, large quantities of olive oil, famous for its excellent quality, were being exported to France, Trieste and Livorno from the ports of the Peloponnese. Nowadays, this region produces a fragrant, fruity olive oil of a magnificent dark green colour. The most famous places in this context are

Harvesting the olives is a lengthy affair, beginning in November in Crete and ending in February. The basic tools have remained the

For larger olive trees where olives where olives are difficult to reach by hand, thin, flexble sticks are used to gently knock the fruit from the tree onto collecting nets which are laid out bellow.

The ideal way of picking olives: by hand and one by one directly from the tree so as to avoid bruises.

After a hard day"s work, the olives are taken to the press.

more modern and mechanical way of harvesting the olives, but there are still people who remain faithful to the old ways, and some even pick their olives by hand, one by one...

THE OLIVE PRESS

The olives, once gathered in special sacks or baskets, are taken to the press where the bits of branches and leaves are oblite-

In modern presses, the branches and leaves are discarded mechanically and the olives are washed before being crushed.

same through out the centuries: flexible twigs with which to gently beat the branches laden with olives, or rakes that carefully "comb" the olives off the trees and onto the nets spread around the tree trunk. Nowadays there is a

rated; they are then washed to get rid of the dust.

CRUSHING OF OLIVES IN THE PAST

One, two, sometimes three millstones, were worked by animal or manpower and put to grind the olives. Horses, or more often strong mules, were made to turn the stones and the olives were crushed under the weight of these gigantic millstones. It was hard work, requiring time and energy.

NOWADAYS

There are two methods. The traditional one still uses millstones, which however are mechanically put in motion, and the

An oldfashioned animal - draw olive mill.

In a modern olive press, granite millstones mechanically cruch olives in a stain less basin.

A hand - worked press working the olive pulp.

The pulp is spun at high speed, thus separating the flesh of the olives from the oil.

A 1950's Greek advertisment for extra virgin olive oil

olives are crushed in a steel basin. The pulp is then separated in thin layers with round synthetic filters in between. An hydraulic press, with a pressure graded between 250 and 400 Kg per square centimetre, brings out the oil from the pulp, lets it run through the filters into containers where it is separated from the water.

The second method is entirely centrifugal: the pulp is spun at high speed and thus separates the flesh of the olives from the oil. Once the oil has been separated from the water, the hundred percent virgin oil obtained is wholly untreated (i.e., virgin).

SINOLEA, THE MODERN TECHNOLOGY

The state-of-the-art method for obtaining oil from the olives is known as sinolea. A significant number of Cretan producers prefer this method because it leaves the fragrance of the oil intact and the quality is first-rate. After crushing the olives and

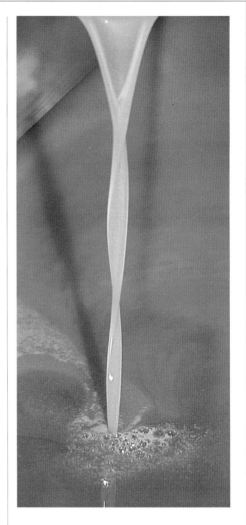

obtaining the paste in a classical manner, small paper-thin crescent-shaped steel blades run quickly and continuously through the paste, maintaining at the same time temperatures below 100 degrees Fahrenheit, which is the maximum allowed in cold pressing.

QUALITY CONTROL

Large bottling companies, and some of the smaller ones, include well-equipped laboratories and highly specialized staff in charge of analyzing at least 25 different samples per olive oil batch. The consumer in this case rests assured that the quality of the oil he/she buys is guaranteed.

PITHARIA: THE LARGE MINOAN STORING JARS

From Minoan times and until recently, olive oil was stored in gigantic clay jars called "pitharia" that were kept in cool, dark storerooms. These "pitharia" are sometimes still used in certain villages and the famous potters in the village of Thrapsano produce similar jars on request.

MODERN STORAGE OF OLIVE OIL

Large steel basins are used nowadays in modern installations to store the olive oil. Samples are regularly taken for analysis. According to the quality, the oil is classified and stored in different basins where the oil is kept for a long time in its original state and quality.

"Pitharia": these enormous jars were found at the Knossos palace and were used in Minoan times to strore the olive oil. This storage system continued for many centuries.

BOTTLING

Although the exact procedures may vary, a sterile environment is indispensable for bottling and the process is fully automated. Modern automated bottling equipment allows for a very slow filling of the bottles, a method that prevents the air from getting into the bottle.

CRETAN ORGANIC OLIVE OIL

The organic method of cultivating olive trees is definitely gaining ground in recent years. The steps taken in this process are specific

and affect the planting of the trees, their disposition, the prevention

and cure of all sorts of diseases; the fertilizer used is made of one

hundred percent natural materials such as animal manure or compost (wild greens, branches, olive leaves and so on).

Whereas this organic method has been implemented in the Peloponnese for many years now, it was only introduced in Crete in 1993. Nowadays there are about 180 organic cultures of olive trees covering a surface of 2.500 square metres.

GREEK ORGANIC OLIVE OIL

Greece produces 500.000 tons of organic olive oil in olive groves that cover a surface of 30.000 square kilometres. Specific, highly specialized organisations are in charge of controlling the quality of the oil produced in this manner.

GRADES OF OLIVE OIL AS DEFINED BY THE INTERNATIONAL OLIVE OIL COUNCIL

VIRGIN OLIVE OIL is the oil obtained from the olives solely by mechanical or other physical means under conditions -and in particular thermal conditions- that prevent alterations in the oil. The olives undergo no other treatment beyond washing, centrifugation and filtration. VIRGIN OLIVE OIL is classified as follows:

- EXTRA VIRGIN OLIVE OIL with an acidity of less than 1%, perfect in taste and smell. This essentially traditional produce is actually the juice made from the first pressing of the olives, keeping all its flavour, fragrance and colour. Technically speaking, extra virgin olive oil has the lowest natural level of free oleic acid.

- CRETAN EXTRA VIRGIN OLIVE OIL is the best olive oil not just in Greece but in all the Mediterranean, with a perfect balance in aroma, taste and colour. Chemically, this Cretan oil is rich in monosaturated acid fats and natural antioxidant factors such as tokopherol and polyphenol. Rich too in vitamins, it is ideal for a healthy diet.

- FINE VIRGIN OLIVE OIL has an acidity of less than 1.5% and is otherwise excellent in taste and aroma.

- SEMI-FINE OLIVE OIL conserves a good taste and aroma and does not exceed 3% in acidity level.

- REFINED OLIVE OIL is a virgin olive oil that has been refined.

- OLIVE OIL or PURE OLIVE OIL is a blend of refined olive oil and virgin olive oil.

ASSESSING OLIVE OIL

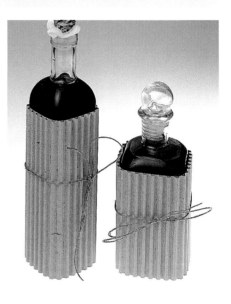

TASTING AT HOME...

Tasting should take place in a neutral well-lit environment. Choose two or three different kinds and take care not to read the labels and thus be influenced. Have a piece of paper and a pen ready to jot down your impressions of taste, fragrance and colour. Eat a little apple between tries to keep your palate clean and don't eat anything for at least one hour before the test. Perfumes and any other cosmetic elements with a strong smell, but also medicine of any kind in particular against the flu', will

Purchase two or three different kinds of olive oil that you can then taste at home. A uniq ue tasting experience that you will find most rewarding and will make you discover a new world of aromas and tastes...

negatively affect your evaluations of the different oils you want to test.

NOTE: the acidity contained in olive oil is not like the one in vinegar or lemons and is only perceptible in oil that has gone bad.

LOOKING AT THE OLIVE OIL

Empty a little olive oil in the flute type of wine glasses and look at the colour holding it up to the light. This may vary greatly, within a same range, from dark green to pale green or to an almost transparent golden shade of green.

Admire the wonderful colours of the different types of olive oil: green for more fruity kinds, goldeny when the olives are large and ripe, slightly blurred in the case of a young olive oil.

IS COLOUR AN INDICATION OF QUALITY?

No, not always. However, as a rule, the greener the oil the stronger the aroma and the richer the taste. This is due to the fact that the olives were picked at exactly the right moment, not too ripe and not too black. But a rich green colour can also be obtained through placing a few leaves from the olive tree when the olives are being pressed; the colour is improved in this manner but not the taste which becomes bitter.

USING YOUR SENSE OF SMELL

The aroma of the oil has to do with the state of the oil. Cradle the

Remember:
smelling is an essential part of olive oil tasting.

glass in your palm and swing the oil to and fro for a couple of times; then take in the smell in a deep breath and analyze your feelings: does it smell fresh, is the smell strong, how can you define it?

TASTING OLIVE OIL

This is the most important step. Take a mouthful of the oil but

Before proceeding to taste another olive oil, remember to clean your palate with a slice of apple.

don't swallow it yet. As in wine tasting, have the liquid circulate in your mouth, over and under your tongue and finally let it slide down your throat, letting the air out through your teeth. Try to evaluate the acidity; is the taste bitter, sweet, sharp? The tongue tastes the bitterness, the inside of the cheeks taste the sharpness and the tip of the tongue, the sweetness.

DO ALL KINDS OF OLIVE OIL TASTE THE SAME?

There is a wide range in the taste of olive oil and it is precisely these natural flavours that make olive oil so unique among other edible oils.

Connoisseurs generally classify olive oil as mild (delicate, light or buttery), semi-fruity (with a stronger taste of olives) and fruity (with a full-blown olive fragrance).

FLAVOURS VARY FROM ONE REGION TO THE NEXT

The climate, the soil, the weather, the harvesting methods, the type of olives, the specific situation of the olive grove, all play a significant role in the final taste of the olive oil. Just as with wine, there is a great difference in taste between all the olive oils produced in Greece, and even between the Cretan kinds. It is up to you to discover them!

FLAVOUR AND AROMA

There is a standard rule applied in countries that produce olive oil to evaluate the quality. Regulation ECC 2568/91 was established on the basis of a general evaluation of the characteristics of olive oil and helps to understand the richness in flavour and aroma. Olive oil connoisseurs can distinguish a great variety in both these factors.

PLEASANT TASTES AND SMELLS

By comparison with other edibles:
- Apple: olive oil reminiscent of the taste of either a ripe apple or else the peel of a green apple
- Grass: a scent like the one of freshly mown grass
- Green leaves: a taste similar to that of unripe olives and leaves
- Almond: a strong taste like the one of a fresh almond
- Hay: a typical smell of some kinds of olive oil that tend to smell like hay
- Fruit: fresh olive oil in particular often has a multiple aroma that brings to mind different types of fresh fruit
  - Lemon: a delicate unusual fragrance with a peppery taste
    - Sorrel: similar to the lemon fragrance, but not as definite
- Spice: some kinds of olive oil leave a pungent, spicy, sweet-'n-sour taste

UNPLEASANT TASTES AND SMELLS
Rush
Earth
Worm
Metal
Mildew
Brine

HOW TO BUY OLIVE OIL

In every important market-place in Greece and throughout Crete, you can find picturesque little shops where a series of traditional products are on sale including, of course, a selection of olive oils from different regions.

WHERE TO FIND IT

In Crete as in the Peloponnese and in the rest of Greece you can find olive oil in different qualities and in an assortment of packages containing smaller or larger quantities of oil. Besides finding olive oil in shops that specialize in local products such as herbs and spice, you can always find some at the super markets and at the Greek airports.

YOU CAN ORDER YOUR OLIVE OIL

For a large amount of olive oil, you can get in touch with the producing and bottling company of your choice. The olive oil will be sent to your address.

WHY IS OLIVE OIL SO EXPENSIVE

Very simply because it is difficult to produce. While sunflower oil and corn oil are easy to produce, good olive oil on the contrary, especially of the best quality, is expensive to produce and demands much work. There is also the fact that every olive tree requires 6 years of continual care to bear fruit.

YOU DONT NEED LARGE QUANTITIES

Because the best quality olive oil is so aromatic and full, a small quantity is enough to enrich your dishes and salads.
One litre of olive oil, of the best quality, lasts for at least 50 to 60 times if you want to use it raw on salads, boiled greens, fish or meat.

HAVE YOU EVER USED OLIVE OIL?

If not, make sure you begin your acquaintance with this product using extra virgin olive oil, which you can use raw on your salad and other dishes: its rich fragrance is in itself a wonderful addition to the best food.

READ THE LABEL

As a rule, the olive oil on sale always has a label in English, indicating the following:
• the acidity
• the area where the specific olive oil is from
• the company producing it
• the name of the region or town of production
• the quantity contained in the bottle
• the bottling date
• the expiry date
• the type of culture (organic or not)

SHAPE AND COLOUR OF BOTTLES

You can find olive oil on sale in a series of bottles or stainless metal cans in a variety of designs and colours. If you buy bottled olive oil, you should choose the darker bottles that protect the oil from the light. However, on the other hand, transparent bottles allow one to see the actual colour of the oil...

TASTING BEFORE BUYING

You are of course entitled to try the olive oil you want to buy, in particular if you are buying it from a Delicatessen store or a shop specializing in local products. Don't hesitate to ask for a sample.

WHAT TO AVOID

• Olive oil that has been left to stand in the sun: better choose one from the shelf inside the store.
• Olive oil badly packed, with a lid that doesn't fit properly: chances are it may have gone bad...
• Olive oil in packaging that

doesn't mention the production area and specific company.

• Olive oil in packaging that doesn't mention the dates of production and expiry.

OLIVE OIL HAS A LIFE LIMIT

Contrary to wine, olive oil has a life limit and is usually at its best for the first 18 to 20 months. Later, it begins to loose its aroma, and in particular olive oil containing spices or aromatic herbs tends to turn acid after a year or so.

HOW DOES OLIVE OIL TRAVEL

It is by no means difficult to take a couple of olive oil bottles with you even if you are travelling far. Again, contrary to wine, movement does not affect the quality of olive oil. It is better to transport the olive oil in glass or metallic packaging, rather than in plastic, and you can ask the shopkeeper to pack it for you for the journey. Place it in your suitcase, and hold it in place with clothes or towels. You can of course carry it as hand-luggage: first-class olive oil, bought in its place of origin is worth the trouble and is not something easily found anywhere else....

HOW TO STORE IT AT HOME

Once you have brought your precious burden oil safely home, store it in a dark and cool place, away from light and especially from heat. The cellar, if you

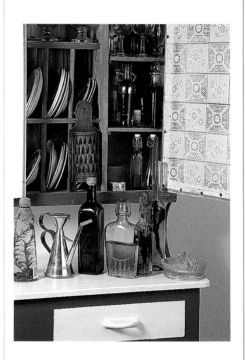

happen to have one, is an ideal storage place for olive oil.

THE REFRIGERATOR

This is not the best place to keep olive oil: cold temperatures will blur and thicken the valuable liquid, even if it does not alter its taste. If left at room-temperature for a couple of hours, it will regain its lovely quality and colour.

WHAT TO FEAR

Olive oil has four enemies:
- light and in particular sun
- high temperatures
- oxygen
- metal

MAKE NOTES

If you like the olive oil you have bought, make sure to keep the label, or else write it down. You can contact the production company whenever you want and they will ship you any amount of olive oil you desire, or else you can

personally buy more of the same kind in your next trip to Greece. Remember to tell your friends what variety pleased you most: in this manner you will help them to make their choice.

EXTRA VIRGIN OLIVE OIL IS THE BEST GIFT

Take your friends and/or relatives a small bottle of olive oil: you can't go wrong, they will be thrilled to receive olive oil directly from the country of origin, the country where the best olive oil is produced.

OTHER GIFTS FROM THE OLIVE TREE

SOAP

You can buy excellent olive oil soap at very good prices in the market. Excellent for skin and hair.

OLIVES

You cannot miss noticing the rich variety of olives: green or black, large or small, in brine or salt, with

or without aromatic herbs (mainly rosemary, thyme or coriander), they look beautiful in their picturesque containers. It is best to buy them loose but you can also find them in packages.

OLIVE PASTE

Olive paste has always been a prized hors-d'oeuvre: simply spread some on a slice of fresh bread, as the Ancient Greeks used to do....

CHEESE KEPT IN OLIVE OIL

The famous cheeses kept in olive oil in larger or smaller jars come mainly from Crete and Mytilene: they have a particularly hot, peppery taste.

AROMATIC OLIVE OIL

Olive oil can be perfumed with the fragrance of different herbs: oregano, sage or rosemary are the best. They come in large and in small bottles.

THE LEAVES FROM THE OLIVE TREE

An excellent beverage to counter high blood pressure. Bring 24 olive leaves to the boil in 8 glasses of water and simmer for a quarter of an hour. Drink this beverage morning and evening for 2 weeks.

THE WOOD OF THE OLIVE TREE

Authentic olive wood is very beautiful. Its colour is a blend of black, brown and honey shades. You can find beautiful household ware made in this wood: salad bowls, boxes, small pieces of furniture, and an assortment of small objects with which to decorate your home.

NATURAL BEAUTY PRODUCTS

There are several companies in Greece using olive oil or olive kernels to produce natural beauty products. On sale at the drug-stores.

COOKING WITH OLIVE OIL

O live oil is an ideal fat for cooking purposes. It gives a wonderful taste to the food and makes it healthier and easier to digest. You can enjoy olive oil in a great variety of recipes, either cooked or raw; excellent for marinading meat or fish, it is ideal too for frying.

WHAT TYPE TO USE

For casserole cooking it is best to use a not too rich variety of olive oil: its volatile elements will not let off too strong a smell in your kitchen. If you want to appreciate the full flavour of the olive oil in all its delicacy, you must add it to your cooking only towards the end. Delicate dishes, such as fish and soups, require a lighter, not too fruity kind of olive oil.

DELICIOUS WAYS TO ENJOY EXTRA VIRGIN OLIVE OIL

• Replace butter or margarine by a little plateful of olive oil in which to dip your bread or rusk.

• Add a tablespoon of olive oil to the water in which you boil your pasta: in this way, it won't stick.

• Rub a little olive oil on your hands to spread your dough to prevent sticking

• Pour a little olive oil over your potatoes before baking them to make them more crisp.

• Sprinkle olive oil on all greens, on boiled potatoes, on carrots, beans or any other vegetable and serve them with fresh parsley and spring onions.

WHAT TO USE TO POUR OLIVE OIL ON YOUR SALAD

While in Greece, think of buying the small bottles called "ladera" or "ladika" or "ladotiria" that you find in most tavernas: the special spout allows the olive oil to flow slowly and you can add the exact amount desired. In this manner, the oil spreads over the salad and impregnates it all with its heavenly taste. These recipients come in a variety of shapes and sizes.

OLIVE OIL AND BAKING

The fine texture of your baking is guaranteed if you use olive oil: this monounsaturated fat has a specific fat crystal which is ideal in baking. It also contains tocopherols (vitamin E) and these act as emulsifiers, producing cakes with a nice crust that are moist tender inside. Tocopherols also have antioxidant qualities that help keep the fresh quality of the baked product. You can replace other fats (oils, butter, margarine) in baking recipes with olive oil. If you are replacing a solid shortening, you must use 25 % less of olive oil. Here are some products that are particularly enhanced through the use of olive oil in the baking process: cookies, cakes (carrot cake, nut cake, fruit tarts and so on), corn bread, muffins, biscuits, scones and pizza.

Small usefull oil conteiners

EQUIVALENT MEASUREMENT TABLE FOR BAKING

Butter or margarine	Olive oil
1 teaspoon	$3/4$ of a teaspoon
1 tablespoon	$2^{1/4}$ teaspoon
2 tablespoons	$1^{1/2}$ tablespoons
$1/4$ cup	3 tablespoons
$1/3$ cup	$1/4$ cup
$1/2$ cup	$1/3$ cup + 2 tablespoons
$2/3$ cup	$1/2$ cup
$3/4$ cup	$3/4$ cup
1 cup	$3/4$ cup

BROILING AND GRILLING

Roasted, barbecued and braised dishes benefit from the use of olive oil which, thanks to the lighter volatile elements it contains, will smell less in your kitchen. Marinading in olive oil, with a shot of vinegar, wine or lemon, brings out the taste of the meat/fish you intend broiling or grilling.

FRYING IN OLIVE OIL

Olive oil increases in volume when heated: therefore you need a smaller quantity to fry, deep fry or sauté your food. Olive oil tends to coat fried food, rather than be absorbed. Deep frying in olive oil produces a crisp crust, sealing in the juices of meat or fish and enhancing the flavour of the vegetables. Olive oil can be filtered after use in frying and reused up to 3 times.

Deep frying in olive oil produces a crisp crust, sealing in the juices.

Food which has been fried in olive oil has been used as many as seven times, is very easily digested. Corn oil and sunflower oil burn at 160º C whereus olive oil burs at a higher temperature at 200º - 200º C

FLAVORED OILS

1. OLIVE OIL FLAVORED WITH ROSEMARY BAY LEAVES AND PINK PEPPERCORNS

This delicate flavored oil is ideal for light marinades for chicken or partridge.
It also gives a special flavor when used to make mayonnaise.

INGREDIENTS

2 cups (500 ml) extra virgin olive oil
1 sprig fresh rosemary
2 fresh bay leaves
1 tsp. pink peppercorns

METHOD

1. Rinse and dry well the herbs on kithen towel.
2. Fill up a clean dry bottle with olive oil .
3. Add the herbs and the peppercorns.
4. Cap the bottle tightly and leave in a cool and dark place for 3 weeks , until ready for use.

2. OLIVE OIL FLAVORED WITH CORIANDER LIME & PINK PEPPERCORNS

INGREDIENTS

2cups (500 ml)
extra virgin olive oil
1 tsp. coriander seeds
1 tsp. green and black peppercorns
1 large strip of lime peel

METHOD

1. Coarsely crush the coriander and peppercorns with a mortar and pestle , or electric grinder.
2. Fill up a clean bottle with olive oil. Add the coriander , peppercorns and lime peal.
3. Cap the bottle tightly and leave in a cool and dark place for 2 - 3 weeks. Once opened, it keeps for up to 4 - 5 months.

Olive oil with rosemary

3. FIVE FLAVORS OLIVE OIL

Ideal for boiled potatos , roast beef or pork , over feta cheese grilled in the oven and dried barley bread.

INGREDIENTS

4 cups extra virgin olive oil
1 sprig fresh rosemary
1 tsp. level dried thyme
1 tsp. level dried oregano
3 fresh mint leaves
4 fresh basil leaves
1 tbsp. sea salt

METHOD

1. Rinse and dry the herbs well, on kitchen towel.
2. Crush them with mortar and pestle or electric grinder, to give off their aroma .
3. Put inside clean and dry bottle. Add olive oil and salt.
4. Cap the bottle tightly and keep in cool and dry place for 3 weeks. Shake once or twice , during storage period.
5. Strain the oil and transfer to clean bottles . Discard the herbs .

Herbs and spice ofte enhance the taste of olive oil, bringing out its fruitness.
You can use this type of oil for your vinaigrette sauce, or simply on plain boiled vegetables.

4. OLIVE OIL WITH DRIED TOMATOES

Only a few drops of this kind of olive oil, may enrich the taste of feta cheese, or halloummi (famous cheese, from Cyprus)grilled in the oven or in a special plate of pasta salad. Use the tomatoes and the caper to make special sauces.

INGREDIENTS

2 cups extra virgin olive oil
6 finely chopped, dried tomatoes
2 tbsp caper

METHOD

1. Buy small tomatoes. Dry the tomatoes well on a kitchen towel and cut them in half or in wedges, if they are large. Put them on a wooden or straw surface. Sprinkle them with plenty of rough salt.
2. Cover them with a thin cotton towel and place them, under the sun until they dry and lose all their liquids. At night, it is better to transfer the tomatoes inside, to avoid humidity. They need 8-12 days to be ready, depending on the sun and the size of the tomatoes. Alternately, arrange the tomatoes in a vase with the caper and fill up with the extra virgin olive oil.
3. Cap the bottle tightly, keeping it in a cool dry place for 2 weeks before use.

5. OLIVE OIL FLAVOURED WITH ROSEMARY BAY LEAVES THYME AND SAGE

Ideal when used to make marinades for partridge and red meat, cooked in the saucepan.

INGREDIENTS

2 cups olive oil
1 sprig fresh rosemary
2 bay leaves
1 tsp dried thyme
1 tsp dried sage leaves

METHOD

1. Brush the rosemary well with a wet kitchen towel and leave to dry well.
2. In a clean glass bottle with a large opening put all the ingredients together.
3. Cap tightly and keep in cool and dark place for 2-3 weeks. Transfer to a clean bottle and throw out the flavored herbs.

6. OLIVE OIL WITH FRESH BASIL AND GARLIC

Ideal for pasta with Mediterranean fish sauce. Add canned anchovy fillets or sardines in brine. It is better to prepare it in small quantities.

INGREDIENTS

2 cups extra virgin olive oil
3 cloves of garlic
1 ½ tbsp fresh basil leaves, finely chopped.
2 grains green pepper

METHOD

1. Fill up a clean bottle or a pot with olive oil, add the garlic, the basil and the green pepper.
2. Cap tightly and keep in a cool and dark place for 2 weeks until ready for use.

7. OLIVE OIL WITH CINNAMON, NUTMEG, CLOVES AND POPPY PETALS

This recipe has been used for curative and medical purposes(sore throat, sufferings, pains) It's a special red olive oil with three aromatic elements intensely , that make it an ideal flavour in olive oil biscuits and cookies.

INGREDIENTS

2 cups extra virgin olive oil
2 pieces of cinnamon wood
1 tsp cloves
1 whole nutmeg
15 poppy petals

METHOD

1. Crush the nutmeg and the cloves in a wooden mortar thoroughly.
2. Put them with the cinnamon and the poppy petals in a clean bottle and fill up with the oil.
3. Cap the bottle tightly and leave it in a cool and dark place for 2-3 weeks before using.

8. OLIVE OIL WITH FENNEL

This flavored olive oil is ideal for boiled and roasted fish also for shells.

INGREDIENTS

2 cups virgin olive oil
1 tbsp fennel, finely chopped
½ tsp fennel seeds, crushed
1 tbsp citron-fruit grated

METHOD

1. Rinse and dry well the citron-fruit.
2. Grate the citron-fruit well with a special tool or a toothed knife.
3. Fill up a clean bottle with olive oil, add the fennel the fennel seeds and the grated citron-fruit.
4. Cap tightly and keep in cool and dark place for 2-3 weeks until ready for use.

9. OLIVE OIL WITH ANISE, CINNAMON, CLOVES

*It can be used for kneading biscuits or sweet breads.
You must be careful, not to leave the olive oil for a long time because it will get a strong unpleasant smell.*

INGREDIENTS

2 cups extra virgin olive oil
1 tsp anise, star-shaped
2 pieces of cinnamon wood
1 tsp cloves

METHOD

1. Put all the spices into a wooden mortar. Crush thoroughly 2-3 times.
2. Empty the mortar in to a pot or jar with a large opening. Fill up with the olive oil, cap the pot tightly and store it in a cool place for 2 weeks. It will only keep for 3-4 months.

10. SAGE OLIVE OIL

Ideal flavoured olive oil for pork or partridge. It also gives a special taste when sprinkled on to salad with boiled potatoes and salted olives.

INGREDIENTS

2 cups extra virgin olive oil, preferably green olive oil - sour oil.
2 branches fresh sage
1 tsp thoroughly rubbed, drained leaves of sage
1 tsp green pepper

METHOD

1. In a clean bottle put the green pepper, the sage leaves, and the branches in vertical position into the bottle.
2. Fill up with the oil, cap tightly and store it for 2-3 weeks in a cool place, until ready to be used.

11. HOT PEPPERS OLIVE OIL

For salads, boiled vegetables, or roast meat it is ideal to use this kind of hot olive oil.

INGREDIENTS

2 cups of extra virgin olive oil
2 dried hot red pepper
1 fresh green hot pepper

METHOD

1. Squeeze the peppers thoroughly and put them in a bottle or jar with a large opening.
2. Fill up with olive oil, cap the bottle tightly and leave for 2-3 weeks in a cool and dark place. Conserved for 3-4 months.

SAUSES AND DRESSINGS

2

1. OLIVE OIL AND LEMON

INGREDIENTS

1/2 cup (125 ml) extra virgin
olive oil
5 tbsp. lemon juice
1 tsp. ready mustard
1 tsp. salt
1 tsp. flour

METHOD

Shake all the ingredients in a jar
with a tight - fitting lid , until
well combined .

2. OLIVE OIL AND LEMON WITH PARSLEY OR DILL

INGREDIENTS

1 cup (250 ml)
extra virgin olive oil
5 tbsp. lemon juice
1/2 cup finely minced
parsley or dill
2 -3 drops warm water
1 level tbp. salt

METHOD

Shake all the ingredients well in a
jar with a tight - fitting lid until
well combined.

3. OLIVE OIL LEMON - VINEGAR AND GARLIC

*The simplest and most popular sauce in Greece. It brings out the
aroma of the fresh vegetables and gives an extra flavour to any
plain dish .*

INGREDIENTS

1/2 cup (125 ml) extra virgin
olive oil
5 tbsp. lemon juice
1 tsp. salt
2 drops warm water

METHOD

Shake all ingredients in a jar
with a tight - fitting lid , until
all combined .

4. OLIVE OIL - VINEGAR AND GARLIC

Ideal accompaniment to fried eggplants

INGREDIENTS

1/2 cup (125 ml) extra virgin olive oil
4 tbsp. vinegar
4 tbsp. lemon juice
4 garlic cloves crushed
1 tsp. salt
1 - 3 drops warm water

METHOD

1. Crush garlic and salt together with mortar and pestle or electric grinder.
2. Transfer to a jar with a tight-fitting lid . Add vinegar, lemon juice and water. Shake well until combined.

5. OLIVE OIL - MINT - MUSTARD AND OREGANO

Tasty topping for boiled eggs

INGREDIENTS

1/2 cup (125 ml) extra virgin olive oil
2 tbsp. vinegar
1 tsp. fresh mint leaves , finely chopped
1 tsp. dried oregano
1 tsp. prepared mustard
1 tbsp. flour
1 tsp. salt
2 - 3 drops warm water

METHOD

1. In a bowl whisk all the ingredients until well combined.
2. Refrigerate covered , for at least 35 - 50 minutes until ready for use.

6. OLIVE OIL - BASIL AND GARLIC

This dressing is an excellent spaghetti sauce , when sardines and anchovies are added.

INGREDIENTS

2 cups (500 ml) extra virgin olive oil
3 garlic cloves crushed
1/2 tbsp. fresh basil leaves, finely chopped
1/2 tsp. green peppercorns

METHOD

1. Fill up a clean bottle with olive oil. Add garlic , basil and peppercorns.
2. Cap tightly and keep in cool and dark place for 2 - 3 weeks until ready for use .

7. OLIVE OIL - GINGER AND FENNEL SEEDS

The aroma and body of this oil makes it ideal for steamed or boiled vegetables.

INGREDIENTS

2 cups (500 ml) extra virgin olive oil
1 tbsp. fresh ginger root , grated
1/3 tsp. fennel seeds , crushed

METHOD

1. Coarsely grind fennel seeds with mortar and pestle or electric grinder.
2. Fill up a clean bottle with olive oil . Add ground fennel seeds , ginger and cap tightly .
3. Keep bottle in cool and dark place for 2 weeks , until ready for use .

8. LEMON FLAVORED OLIVE OIL

INGREDIENTS

½ cup extra virgin olive oil
5 tbsp lemon juice
1 tsp salt
2 drops warm water

METHOD

1. Put all the ingredients in a large bowl or in a glass jar with a tight – fitting lid, shake until well combined.

9. OLIVE OIL - OREGANO AND HONEY

Ideal for roast or smoked pork.

INGREDIENTS

3/4 cup (180 ml) extra virgin olive oil
1 tsp. dried thyme
1 tsp. oregano
1/2 tbsp. honey
1 tbsp. lemon juice
2 - 3 drops warm water

METHOD

1.   Whisk well in a bowl , olive oil , honey , lemon juice and water , until combined .
2.   Add thyme and oregano and fold in for about 3- 4 minutes.

10. GREEN GARLIC SAUCE

This is a perfect accompaniment to small fried fish , or cooked meat. Parsley gives this sauce a beautiful green color.

INGREDIENTS

1 cup (250 ml)
extra virgin olive oil
3 medium potatoes boiled , peeled and cut in pieces
4 garlic cloves ,crushed
5 tbsp. strong wine vinegar
Salt
Parsley leaves and olives for garnish

METHOD

1.   Blend the garlic and parsley in a food processor with 2 - 3 quick turns.
2.   Drop potatoes piece by piece through feed tube , making sure each piece has been completely mixed before adding more .
3.   Add gradually one after the other oil and vinegar.
4.   Adjust salt and extra vinegar , according to taste.
5.   Serve in a bowl and garnish with parsley leaves and olives.

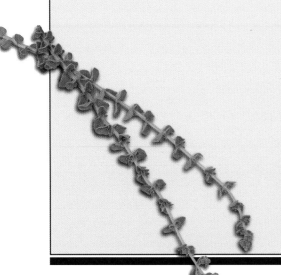

Green garlic sauce and fried atichokes

11. OLIVE OIL WITH BAKED GARLIC CLOVES AND ONIONS

Distribute this olive oil sauce in to saucers (or small plates) and put them in the middle of the table. Serve them before the first plate with various small bread buns for your guests to dip in.

INGREDIENTS

2 cups of extra virgin olive oil
1 garlic clove
1 medium onion
1 tsp brown sugar
1 tsp salt

METHOD

1. Clear the exterior peel and cut off the head of the garlic without separating the cloves. Leave the onion unpeeled.
2. Put the garlic and the onion, in the center of a separate piece of aluminum foil. Sprinkle with the sugar and the salt, pour olive oil around with a table spoon, fold and bake in the grill at high temperature, for 15-20 minutes.
3. Open the foil and let the garlic and the onion cool. Put them into a glass pot and fill up with the olive oil. Cap tightly and let the oil to "obtain" it's aromas for at least 1-2 days.

12. HOT CHILI WITH RED PEPPER AND CHEESE

Put this hot sauce in small plates at the center of the table and serve before the main dish. Accompany them with black wheat bread or barley dried bread.

INGREDIENTS

1 cup extra virgin olive oil
1 cup sour soft cheese(mysithra)
1 tsp fresh finely chopped mint
1 tsp finely chopped hot red pepper
1 tsp tomato paste
A pinch of freshly ground black pepper
A pinch of cumin

METHOD

1. Whisk the eggs in a large bowl, then add the olive oil with the tomato paste and one table spoon of warm water.
2. Add the mint, the hot red chili, the black pepper, the cumin and finally the sour soft cheese. Stir all the ingredients until well combined and the mixture becomes thick.
3. Transfer it into small bowls and store in the fridge for 3-4 hours for the ingredients to release their aromas.

13. OLIVE OIL FLAVORED WITH PAPRIKA AND CRUSHED CRESS CORNS.

When the spices and the seeds are heated, it brings out their aroma. Served with small bread buns.

INGREDIENTS

1 cup extra virgin olive oil
1 tbsp paprika seeds
1 tsp whole cress

METHOD

1. Put the cress seeds in a mortar and crush them thoroughly.
2. Heat a nonstick skillet, add the cress with the paprika. Cook at high temperature for 3-4 minutes, take care not to burn.
3. Transfer them in a clean glass jar and fill up the olive oil immediately.
4. Cap tightly and leave it for 8-10 hours for the oil, to absorb all the flavour.

14. OLIVE OIL WITH DRIED TOMATOES FOR ROAST MEAT.

Ideal to accompany roast lamb or chicken. It also gives a special flavour when used for pasta sauces.
It's possible to use dried tomatoes, soaked for at least 1 hour in warm water, but it's possible to prepare this kind of sauce if you use dried tomatoes conserved in olive oil.
It is optional to add a small hot pepper or paprika.

INGREDIENTS

5 tbsp of extra virgin olive oil
8 pieces of dried tomatoes
2 garlic cloves coarsely crushed
1 medium tbsp basil
salt

METHOD

1. Blend all the ingredients in the food processor in 3-4 quick turns.
2. Taste the sauce if necessary, mix well for 2-3 more medium turns, until combined into a soft mixture.
3. Transfer the sauce into a open serving bowl and serve immediately before cold.

15. OLIVE OIL FLAVOURED WITH ROSE PETALS, NUTMEG AND CLOVES

The name "cloves" result from the Byzantium, it is the same thing as the aromatic cloves, known as carnation or pink. It is an excellent mixture.
Chose an excellent virgin olive oil with a sweet taste, without fruit flavours and never use sour oil.

INGREDIENTS

1 cup olive oil
1 tbsp dried aromatics rose petals
1 whole nutmeg
3 cloves

METHOD

1. Heat on high in a skillet for 4-5 minutes, adding the nutmeg, the cloves and the rose petals. Mix continuously and be careful it doesn't become dark.
2. Transfer the spices while hot, in to a glass pot and fill up with the olive oil immediately.
3. Cap and let season to taste at least 8 hours before serving.

16. OLIVE OIL WITH MARJORAM, SAGE AND "LOVE'S PLANT" (DICTAMO)

This is a really strong flavoured olive oil. The aroma becomes even stronger if the plants are fresh. Leave the aromatic plants in the bowl, when serving the oil.

INGREDIENTS

2 cups olive oil
3-4 leaves of the "love's plant" Dictamo
2-3 leaves of sage
2 pieces of fresh marjoram

METHOD

1. Put the aromatics herbs in a clean glass pot and fill up with the olive oil.
2. Conserve it, in a cool place for 6-7 days before use.

17. SIMPLE OLIVE OIL VINEGAR

It brings out the aroma of the vinegar from the red wine and gives an extra flavour to any plain dish.

INGREDIENTS

1 cup olive oil
½ cup from red wine vinegar
½ tsp salt
2-3 drops warm water

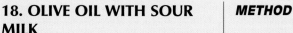

METHOD

1. Shake all the ingredients in a jar with a tight – fitting lid, until well combined.

18. OLIVE OIL WITH SOUR MILK

Put the sauce in small bowls in the middle of the table for your guests to dip in the fried courgettes (zucchini), aubergines and peppers.

INGREDIENTS

4 tbsp extra virgin olive oil
1 cup sour milk
4 garlic cloves
1 tsp mint finely chopped
salt

METHOD

1. Pulpify the garlic and the salt together with the mortar and pestle or electric grinder.
2. Transfer this mixture into a bowl, add the sour milk, the olive oil and the mint.
3. Whisk well with the a fork or the whisker for 2-3 minutes.
4. Cover with foil and keep refrigerated for 2-3 hours, before ready to use. Serve the sauce with fried courgettes, aubergine and fried potatoes.

19. HOME MADE MAYONNAISE WITH OLIVE OIL

Probably the most popular sauce in the Mediterranean and it is at the same time the sauce with the most numerous and interesting of varieties.

The traditional mode of preparation is by hand, not electric grinder, or blender. It is better to prepare it with a heavy fork or a metallic whisker. All the ingredients must be at room temperature and especially the eggs. You must pour the olive oil and the lemon juice drop by drop, while whisking continuously always the same direction. May refrigerate covered, for at least 7-8 days in a bowl.

INGREDIENTS

1 cup extra virgin olive oil
2 yolks
1 tsp salt
1 tsp sugar
1 tbsp vinegar
juice of a medium lemon

METHOD

1. In a deep glass or porcelain - china bowl whisk the eggs with the sugar and the salt continuously, always in the same direction, adding the vinegar little by little.
2. Continue with the olive oil, drop by drop, when the mayonnaise becomes thickened, add the lemon juice gradually and continue in the same mode, stir the oil and the lemon juice one after the other, until the ingredients finish.

20. "PESTO SAUCE" OLIVE OIL WITH BASIL, MARSH-MINT AND ORANGE

A "sensitive" and at the same time "aggressive" sauce, ideal for green salads, or spaghetti. A great way to use this sauce is to put it under the skin of a big chicken to fill the space. Tie the chicken and bake it for about 1 hour. The chicken will obtain an excellent taste.

INGREDIENTS

1 cup extra virgin olive oil
1 cup fresh basil finely chopped
½ cup fresh mint finely chopped
½ cup walnuts
2 tbsp grated fresh orange
2 garlic cloves
½ tsp salt
½ tsp green pepper

METHOD

1. Blend the walnuts, the basil, the mint and the garlic, in food processor at medium speed, until thickened.
2. While the electric grinder is in operation, add the olive oil, the orange, the salt and the pepper gradually.
3. When the ingredients have absorbed the oil, stop the grinder and taste the sauce.
4. If it is very thick, add 1-2 tbsp more olive oil and blend for another 2-3 minutes.

21. "ALIOLI" SAUCE

A light variety of "scordalia" sauce with a different taste. It is customary in Italy and the Ionian Islands. Keep covered and refrigerated, for at least 4-5 days. Ideal accompaniment for fried vegetables, roast meat or fish.

INGREDIENTS

1 cup exra virgin olive oil
5 garlic cloves
2 egg yolks
1 tbsp vinegar from white wine
½ tsp salt

METHOD

1. In a mortar, blend the garlic and the salt well.
2. Transfer the mixture into an electric grinder, adding the vinegar and the eggs thoroughly whisked.
3. Turn on, at low speed and pour in the olive oil drop by drop, until it finishes and the sauce starts thickening.

3

SNACKS AND STARTERS

1. BARLEY RUSKS WITH OLIVE OIL (PAXIMADIA)

This is one of the most popular , classic small snacks in Crete. It is called , the "Cretan owl" named after the round rusks that, resemble the head of an owl. The recipe below is typical of the area of Rethimno . In other areas of Crete this recipe is made without feta cheese . In all cases anyway , it is important to use very fruity flavored olive oil .

INGREDIENTS

4 barley rusks
8 tbsp. extra virgin olive oil
2 large ripe tomatoes , deseeded and cut in small cubes
1 cup hard feta cheese , grated
Salt

METHOD

1. Moisten the rusks with cold water.
2. Drizzle the olive oil over the top and let the rusks absorb it .
3. Salt according to taste . Be especially careful if feta cheese is salty.
4. Arrange the tomato cubes on the rusks. Sprinkle with grated feta cheese and serve.

Barley rusks covered in fresh tomato and virgin olive oil. You can also add a little spring onion and finely chopped parsley.

Dried barley bread absorbs olive oil very well and tastes perfect with fresh tomatoes, feta cheese, garlic and fish roe.

2. SALTED FISH ROE PASTE SALAD

An interesting version of the classic salted fish roe paste, that is prepared only with olive oil and the paste of the salted fish roe. The secret is to blend well and for a long time, so, it becomes soft and velvety.

INGREDIENTS

2 tbsp white of salted fish roe paste (or pink, according to taste)
1-1 ½ cup extra virgin olive oil
1-2 juice of one big lemon

METHOD

1. Blend the paste, at medium speed and gradually add the lemon and the oil.
2. When the mixture becomes smooth and has absorbed all the oil, taste and adjust with the lemon if necessary.
3. Serve the salad paste, in small bowls and garnish with some olives.

3. FRIED BLACK OLIVES WITH ONIONS

INGREDIENTS

2 1/2 cups black olives
1 large onion , cut in fine rings
1 tsp. dried thyme
1 tsp. dried oregano
1 cup (250 ml) extra virgin olive oil

METHOD

1. Soak olives for 12 hours. Rinse , pat dry on kitchen paper .
2. Heat oil in large deep skillet and fry onions until translucent.
3. Add olives and fry for 4 - 6 minutes . Empty the skillet into a strainer .
4. Sprinkle with thyme and oregano. Mix well.
    Serve hot.
    Keep refrigerated if serving cold .

4. CAULIFLOWER IN OLIVE OIL

A crunchy vegetable to be eaten alone or to accompany other fresh salads.

INGREDIENTS

3 cups (750 ml) olive oil
1 large cauliflower , cut into florets
2 dried bay leaves
3 cups white wine vinegar
2 cups white wine
6 - 8 peppercorns
3 - 4 strips of lemon peel
1 tbsp. salt

METHOD

1. Wash cauliflower well , strain and let dry between 2 cloth towels .

2. In a large saucepan , boil water , vinegar , wine , bay leaves, salt and lemon strips.

3. Add cauliflower florets and boil on low heat for a further 5 minutes .

4. Remove cauliflower with slotted spoon and let dry and cool on cloth towel .

5. Place florets in a clean , dry jar, add peppercorns and cover with olive oil. Leave to soak for 10 minutes and if required, add further oil to make sure vegetables are completely covered.

Store in cool and dry place .

5. AUBERGINE IN OLIVE OIL

INGREDIENTS

3 cups extra virgin olive oil
1 kg aubergine
10 basil leaves
2 garlic cloves
2 cups vinegar from red wine
1 heaped tsp salt
black pepper

METHOD

1. Wash and dry the aubergine well on kitchen towel.
2. Cut in slices ½ cm thick. Salt, very well, strain for at least 14 hours to lose the moisture.
3. Boil the vinegar and add the aubergine only for 1 min. Remove with a slotted spoon and strain them.
4. Put in clean large glass jars alternately with the basil leaves, garlic and pepper. Cover with the olive oil.
5. Cap the jars tightly and leave in a cool dark place for 2 weeks before use. Maintain for 4-5 months.

6. SPICY CHEESE BALLS WITH OLIVE OIL AND SOFT CHEESE (MISITHRA OR RICOTTA).

INGREDIENTS

2 cups extra virgin olive oil
½ kg strained sweet soft cheese(misithra or ricotta)
½ kg sour soft cheese
1 tsp ground green pepper
½ tsp red sweet ground pepper
1 tsp fresh basil finely chopped
1 tsp fresh mint finely chopped

METHOD

1. In a bowl mix the two kinds of cheese and all the spices, by hand.
2. When mixed well, form small balls, refrigerate for 24 hours and then drain their liquids by squeezing them.
3. Arrange the balls of cheese in a large open glass jar , and fill up with the olive oil.
4. Keep the small balls of cheese refrigerated 1-2 weeks before use.
5. Maintain them in the fridge for 3-4 months only.

Olive Oil
EAT BETTER, LIVE LONGER

7. OILY BREAD

INGREDIENTS

1 roll of bread / French bread,
stale(2 days old) with not too
much crust
12 tbsp extra virgin olive oil
coarse sea salt
oregano (optional, according to
taste)

METHOD

1. Remove the crust from the
   bread and keep only the
   soft part, cut that in to
   small pieces.
2. Place in a deep bowl and
   drizzle the bread with lots
   of olive oil and the salt.
3. Serve with olives and
   tomatoes cut in to four
   wedges as garnish.

8. GREEN FRIED TOMATOES

*The green unripe tomatoes are
one of the most tasty delicacies, if
fried in plenty of olive oil.
A crunchy vegetable to be eaten
alone, but it is an ideal
accompaniment for a legume
dish.*

INGREDIENTS

10 medium unripe tomatoes
sliced
1 cup of flour
1 ½ cup olive oil
salt

*A simple appetizer
made with tomato
paste and olive oil
drizzled in top*

METHOD

1. Wash, dry and slice the tomatoes and empty into a strainer.
2. Salt the tomatoes and leave for 20-30 minutes to strain their juices.
3. Coat with flour and fry in plenty hot oil until golden. Place each piece on kitchen paper to absorb excess oil and continue to fry until all the slices are used. Serve immediately.

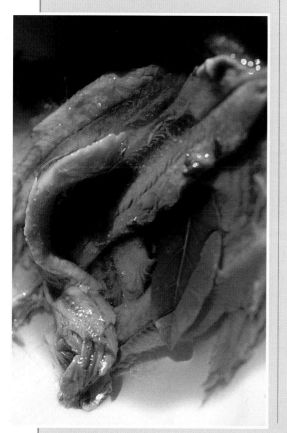

9. SARDINES IN OLIVE OIL

INGREDIENTS

3 cups olive oil
1 kg medium size sardines
2 cups vinegar
1 tbsp fine salt

METHOD

1. Wash the sardines and clean removing the intestines and the heads. Strain them for at least 2-3 hours.
2. Salt and transfer into a narrow bowl. Fill with the vinegar, cover with a plate and leave for 4 hours.
3. Strain from the vinegar and with a small knife open them lengthwise to subtract the middle fish bone.
4. Season the sardines again with vinegar and leave them for another 5 hours until they whiten.
5. Transfer from the vinegar and let them dry thoroughly, on absorbent kitchen towel paper and then arrange the sardines into glass jars.
6. Fill up with the olive oil and keep refrigerated or in a cool place. Maintain them for 5-6 months.

10. FETA CHEESE IN OLIVE OIL

INGREDIENTS

2 cups (500 ml) extra virgin olive oil
1/2 kilo (1 pound) hard feta cheese , cut in cubes
1 tbsp. mustard seeds
1 bay leaf
4 - 5 peppercorns
1 small hot chili pepper

METHOD

1. Coarsely crush mustard seeds and pepper corns , with mortar and pestle or electric grinder.
2. Place feta cheese cubes in a jar. Sprinkle with spice mixture. Add chilli and fill up with olive oil. Keep refrigerated for one week before ready to use.

Generation after generation have daily consumed olives and olive oil

Artichokes with crushed green olives

4

SALADS

1. GREEK SALAD

INGREDIENTS

4 tomatoes , cut in wedges
1 cucumber unpeeled , cut in
rounds
1 green pepper , cut in rings
1 large onion , cut in fine wedges
2 tbsp. capers
1 tsp. dried oregano
15 - 20 black olives

FOR THE DRESSING

1/2 cup extra virgin olive oil
2 tbsp. red wine vinegar
(optional, according to taste)
Salt
Pepper

METHOD

1. In a large open serving bowl
    mix tomatoes , cucumber.,
    onion , pepper as prepared .
2. Add olives and capers .
3. Shake all the ingredients of
    the dressing in a jar with a
    tight fitting lid. Drizzle
    dressing over salad.
    Sprinkle with oregano and
    serve.

The famous "Greek Salad".
Its classical Ingredients:
fresh tomato, cucumbers, capers, onion,
feta cheese, many olives and at least two
or three spoonfuls of oliveoil

2. BAKED POTATO SALAD WITH BLACK OLIVES

INGREDIENTS

3 large potatoes in their jackets
3 large onions , whole and unpeeled
20 black olives
3 tbsp. extra virgin olive oil
Lemon or vinegar (according to taste)
Salt

METHOD

1. Wrap together potatoes and onions in aluminium foil and close it tightly.
2. Bake in oven until soft (approx. 45 minutes depending on size) . Cool .
3. Peel potatoes and onions and cut them in cubes .
4. Serve in large open serving bowl . Season and add olives.
5. Drizzle olive oil and lemon on top (or vinegar if used) .
    Serve hot .

Baked potato salad with olives: an original dish from the Cretan cuisine, an ideal first dish

3. CHICKEN LIVER SALAD

INGREDIENTS

10 chicken livers
1 kilo (2 pounds) mountain greens (fennel, spinach, cress)
1 bunch of rocket
2 tbsp. dill , finely chopped
2 spring onions, cut in fine rings
2 cloves garlic , crushed
Juice of 2 lemons
1 cup green olives , crushed and pitted
3 tbsp. red wine vinegar
3/4 cup (180 ml) extra virgin olive oil (keep 2 - 3 tbsp. for dressing)
Salt
Pepper

METHOD

1. Mix lemon juice , garlic , wine, salt , pepper and marinade chicken livers for at least 3 hours. Drain . Keep marinade aside .
2. In a large skillet , heat oil and sauté drained livers .
3. Add marinade and simmer for 7 - 10 minutes.
4. Mix in a large serving bowl , greens, onions,rocket, and dill. Add livers and olives .
5. Drizzle with remaining oil and vinegar. Season to taste. Serve immediately

4. MIXED LEGUMES SALAD

INGREDIENTS

3/4 cup black eyed beans
3/4 cup small fava beans
3/4 cup broad beans
3/4 cup chick peas
3/4 cup wheat
1 tbsp. salt
1 cup (250 ml) extra virgin olive oil
1/2 cup (180 ml) lemon juice or vinegar according to taste

METHOD

1. Soak beans separately overnight , or at least 8 hours.
2. Rinse thoroughly.
3. In a large saucepan , boil the wheat for 20 minutes . Set aside .
4. Change the water and boil fava beans . Strain and set aside .
5. Change the water and boil together broad beans and chick peas . Strain and set aside .
6. Fill up the pot and boil the water . Salt and add the legumes together , plus the black eyed beans . Boil on high , until soft . Strain and dry. Serve in large open serving bowl and drizzle with olive oil , lemon or vinegar .

5. SALAD WITH FENNEL AND ORANGE

INGREDIENTS

1 large romaine lettuce ,finely shredded
1 large fennel bulb, finely sliced
1 large orange, pealed, cut in fine rounds

FOR THE DRESSING

1/2 cup (125ml) extra virgin fruity olive oil
juice of the large lemon
1 tsp honey
salt
freshly ground pepper

METHOD

1. Wash well and dry, vegetables. Cut as required.
2. Arrange shredded lettuce on a serving plate. Cover with fennel slices. Arrange orange rounds in the centre of the fennel slices.
3. Shake all the dressing ingredients in a jar with a tight - fitting lid until well commbined.
4. Drizzle dressing on salad and serve.

*Above: salad and pulses, an interesting and very healthy Cretan mixture.
Below: Another typical dish requiring plenty of olive oil: "black-eyed" beans and rice.*

6. SALAD WITH BOILED ARTICHOKES

INGREDIENTS

6 large artichokes
6 garlic cloves
2 tbsp dill finely chopped
6 tbsp olive oil
juice from two large lemons
salt, pepper

METHOD

1. Clean the artichokes and keep whole the "hearts".
2. Sprinkle them with the juice to avoid the blackness, open the remaining leaves carefully. Take away the fluff with a penknife.
3. Finely chop the garlic, mix it with the dill and fill the "hearts" of the artichokes with this filling.
4. Arrange them in a narrow deep skillet, add water only to cover. Boil on high for 10-12 minutes.
5. Transfer the artichokes into a large serving bowl, cut in to four pieces one by one and drizzle with lemon olive oil. Season with salt and pepper. Serve hot or warm.

7. SALAD WITH CARROTS AND YOGURT

INGREDIENTS

1 kg large carrots
1 kg strained yogurt,
4 tbsp olive oil
1 crushed garlic cloves,
1 small ripe sliced tomato,
1 cucumber unpeeled, and sliced
1 medium onion, finely sliced
salt

METHOD

1. Wash the carrots well, peel them and boil in plenty of salted water, until soft.
2. Remove with slotted spoon, strain and dry until cool. Grate them lengthways to make thin oblong pieces. Whisk the yogurt well with the olive oil and the salt.
3. Add the garlic and pour yogurt around the carrots. Decorate with the tomato slices, the cucumber, and onion. Serve lightly cold.

8. DRIED BREAD SALAD

Crunchy appetizer that can be used in all the types of fresh salads for more taste.

INGREDIENTS

1 cup extra virgin olive oil
7 slices wheat dried stale bread
4 large ripe tomatoes finely chopped
1 medium onion finely chopped
1 tbsp fresh basil finely chopped
1 large endive
1 bunch rocket finely chopped
3 tbsp vinegar from red wine, salt

METHOD

1. Arrange the slices in a small baking dish or in an oven proof dish, sprinkle with the salt and pour 4 tbsp olive oil around with.

2. Bake in warm to medium heat oven for about 30 min. until gently golden.

3. Remove the baking dish from the oven and let the bread cool completely.

4. In a bowl mix the rocket and the endive. In another bowl mix well the tomato with the bread, the onion and the basil, arrange this mixture over the first mixture with the endive and the rocket.

5. Whisk the rest of the olive oil, the salt and the vinegar well and transfer into an airtight glass jar. Pour this dressing on the salad.

6. Mix all together and serve the salad immediately.

9. SALAD WITH THREE KINDS OF PEPPERCORNS

INGREDIENTS

2 red peppers
2 green peppers
2 yellow peppers
2 garlic cloves crushed
5 tbsp extra virgin olive oil
1 ½ tbsp vinegar
1 level tsp salt

METHOD

1. Take away the stems of the peppers, cutting with a pointed knife all around to remove the seeds.
2. Put the whole peppers in the oven and grill them at a medium temperature until they swell and blacken their peel.
3. Remove from the oven and put them on kitchen towel for 4-5 minutes. Then transfer the peppers in to a plastic bag and close tightly for 10 minutes, so that it will inflate their peel well. Remove the peel with a pointed knife.
4. Cut their flesh in strips with a width of 2-3 cm and put on a serving bowl, sprinkle with the salt. Whisk well, the olive oil, the vinegar and the garlic with a heavy fork.
5. Pour the sauce around, cover them with cling film and leave to marianate for 2-3 hours before serving.

10. BEET ROOTS WITH SOFT CHEESE AND OLIVE OIL

INGREDIENTS

12 large beet roots without the leaves
1 ½ cup of soft sweet cheese (mizithra or ricotta)
4 powdered or grated green peppercorns
4 powdered pink peppercorns
6 tbsp extra virgin olive oil
2 tbsp vinegar from white wine
salt, very small quantity of black pepper

METHOD

1. Boil the beet roots in plenty of salted water until they become soft.
2. Remove them with a slotted spoon and let them dry and cool completely. Keep a cup of their broth aside.
3. Cut the beet roots in thin slices ½ -1 cm. and put aside.
4. In a blender or better in a bowl, whisk the soft cheese (mizithra) well with a fork, with half of the quantity of the green and pink peppecorns and a little salt, until the mixture thickens.
5. Put one of the slices, on a plate to form the base and spread on a part of the soft mixture. Continue to put slices and mixture alternately.
6. You must use 5 similar sized slices of beetroot to create this dish.
7. In a small jar with a tight fitting lid, shake well until the vinegar, the olive oil and the salt have combined. Put 2-3 of these "turrets" in the middle of a white plate.
8. Pour the sauce of the vinegar around. Drip 2-3 drops of the red broth, which has been kept aside, around the plate into the sauce. Sprinkle a little fresh ground pepper around the plate and serve immediately.

Legumes cooked in olive oil are taster and lighter on the stomach

5

VEGETABLES AND BEANS

1. POTATOES IN OIL AND OREGANO

INGREDIENTS

1 cup (250 ml) extra virgin olive oil
1 1/2 kilo (3 pounds) potatoes
1/2 cup (180 ml) fresh lemon juice
1 tsp. dried oregano
1/2 tsp. black pepper
1 tbsp. salt
1 1/2 cup (425 ml) water

METHOD

1. Peel potatoes , cut in wedges , wash and strain .
2. Season with salt and pepper, sprinkle with oregano .
3. Drizzle with 5 - 6 tbsp. olive oil and lemon juice .Pat with hands to press spices on potatoes.
4. Arrange in oven proof dish . Drizzle with remaining olive oil . Add water and bake in preheated oven for 55 - 60 minutes .

2. BLACK EYED BEANS AND RICE

INGREDIENTS

1 cup (250 ml) extra virgin olive oil
1 large onion , grated
1 cup black eyed beans , soaked for 20 - 30 minutes
2 cups rice (do not use parboiled rice)
7 cups water
Juice of half lemon
Salt
Pepper
Lemon wedges for garnish

METHOD

1. Boil beans in plenty of water for 20 minutes.
   Strain.
2. Heat the oil in a saucepan and sauté onions for 3 - 4 minutes , until translucent . Add beans , mix thoroughly and simmer for a further 6 - 8 minutes .
3. Add 7 cups of water and rice.
   Season .

4. Remove from heat and add lemon juice and pepper. Cover saucepan with cotton towel and leave up to 10 minutes , until the mixture becomes moist .
    Season with extra pepper.
    Garnish with lemon wedges.
    Serve warm.

*Above: a classical lentil soup.
Below: "chondros"
(coarsely ground wheat)
simmered with fresh tomato
and olive oil.*

3. CRACKED WHEAT (CHONDROS) IN OLIVE OIL

INGREDIENTS

3/4 cup (180 ml) extra virgin olive oil
2 cups cracked wheat (Chondros)
1 medium onion , finely chopped
2 ripe tomatoes , cut in cubes
(1 1/2 cup tubes)
7 cups water
Salt
Freshly ground pepper

METHOD

1. Heat oil in large saucepan. Add onion and tomatoes , mix thoroughly and sauté gently for 5 - 6 minutes .
2. Add 3/4 cup water, salt and simmer covered for a further 10 minutes.
3. Add cracked wheat , 7 cups of water and boil slowly , uncovered , for 25 minutes , until all water is absorbed.
4. Remove from heat and cover with a cloth for 10 minutes to allow wheat to absorb moisture.

Serve hot with extra freshly ground pepper.

4. FRIED ARTICHOKES

INGREDIENTS

1 1/2 cup (375 ml) olive oil
12 small artichoke hearts
2 cups all purpose flour
2 eggs , separated
3 tbsp. dry white wine
3 tbsp. water
Salt
Pepper
Lemon wedges for garnish

METHOD

1. Boil artichokes in plenty of salted water for 6 - 8 minutes.
    Remove with slotted spoon. Strain and dry.
2. Whisk together egg yolks , wine , water , salt and pepper.
3. Gradually add flour , mixing continuously until smooth.
4. Beat egg whites until stiff peaks form. Fold in the flour mixture with a wooden spoon .
5. Dip the artichokes in the mixture and fry in hot oil.

Serve with lemon wedges as garnish.

5. ROASTED MINT TOMATOES

INGREDIENTS

5 large ripe tomatoes , cut into 1 cm. slices
2 spring onions , finely sliced
1 tbsp. fresh mint leaves , finely minced
2 garlic cloves , finely sliced
2 tbsp. grated cheese (Parmesan or Pecorino)
1 cup (250 ml) olive oil
Salt
Pepper

METHOD

1. Wash , dry and cut the tomatoes. Arrange them in an oven proof dish and season well.
2. Mix onions, garlic, mint . Sprinkle the mixture over the tomatoes.
    Drizzle with oil and bake for 40 - 45 minutes in oven, at 180ºC / 350ºF/ Gas Mark 4
3. Remove from oven and sprinkle with grated cheese.
4. Bake for a further 10 minutes until golden brown on top.

Okra, beans zucchini and aubergines are among the favourite summer
vegetables and are generally cooked with meat, fish or potatoes with,
in every case, a generous amount of olive oil.

6. OKRA AND POTATO RAGOUT

INGREDIENTS

3/4 cup (180 ml) olive oil
1 kilo (2 pounds) okra
2 large potatoes , cut in quarters
3 cups water
1 large onion , finely sliced
2 large ripe tomatoes , cubed
2 tbsp. parsley , finely minced
Juice of 1 lemon
Salt
Pepper

METHOD

1. Clean and wash the
    okra well.
    Cut in half , lengthwise if
    large.
    Drain and salt.
2. In a large saucepan heat
    the oil and sauté the
    onion until golden.
    Add potatoes and 2 cups of
    water.
    Simmer covered for 25
    minutes.
3. Add 1 cup water , okra ,
    parsley and tomatoes. Cook
    gently for a further 15
    minutes.
    Increase heat and cook for
    15 - 20 minutes ,
    uncovered.

Five minutes before cooking
is completed , add lemon
juice. Shake saucepan (do
not use a spoon) .
Let stand for 8 minutes
before serving.
If serving cold , refrigerate.

7. STEW OF CELERY ROOTS AND GREEN PEA

INGREDIENTS

1 cup extra virgin olive oil
1 kg celery roots
2 large onions finely chopped
1 large potato cut in cubes
1 carrot cut in slices
1 cup green pea
1 tbsp dill finely chopped
½ tsp sugar
juice of 2 medium lemons
salt, fresh ground pepper

METHOD

1. Clean the celery roots and
    keep the hearts (the part
    inside the vegetable).
2. Cut in to pieces and boil for
    15 minutes in salted water,
    with the juice of one lemon.
    Remove from the heat and
    strain.
3. Heat the oil in a saucepan
    and sauté the onions until
    translucent. Drop in the

Fresh broad beans and artichokes with olive oil and lemon sause

potatoes the carrots, the celery roots with 1 ½ cups of water, simmer covered for 20 minutes. Arrange the pea, the dill and continue to cook for a further 10 minutes.

5. Dissolve the sugar into the other juice of one lemon and add to the food. Shake the sauce pan gently and taste, add salt and pepper according to taste. Let boil for a further 10' minutes uncovered.

Serve hot or at room temperature.

8. FASTING MOUSAKA
(A DISH OF VEGETABLES COOKED IN THE OVEN)

INGREDIENTS

2 cups common virgin olive oil
5 large potatoes, cut in thin slices
2 large onions cut in thin slices
3 large ripe tomatoes finely chopped
1 tsp tomato paste
1 bunch parsley finely chopped
1/2 cup white wine
2 cups cruched dried bread
salt, pepper

METHOD

1. Deep fry the potatoes in plenty of olive oil. Place them on kitchen paper to absorb excess oil and continue to fry the onions until gently golden, taking care not to burn.

2. Strain all the remaining oil and add the wine to the tomato and the parsley. Season with the salt and pepper mix and simmer for about 15 minutes.

3. Remove the sauce from the heat and throw in one cup of grated toast. Whisk well with a fork, to mix all the ingredients.

4. In a medium size lightly oiled, baking dish, or oven proof tray sprinkle the base with the grated toast and lay in the potatoes, pour over half of the mixture and repeat the layers of potatoes and sauce until the ingredients are finished. It is better to finish the layers with the potatoes.

5. Whisk well the tomato paste with 3-4 tbsp olive oil and spread over the potatoes, sprinkle lots of parsley and a little grated toast on top, bake at 180ºC for about 35 minutes until golden, serve immediately.

9. AUBERGINE WITH RICE AND MINT

INGREDIENTS

1 cup extra virgin olive oil
1 kg aubergine, cut in small pieces
1 ½ cup rice
1 large onion finely grated
1 large ripe tomato cut in cubes
1 tbsp fresh mint finely chopped
1 tbsp salt
freshly ground pepper

METHOD

1. Put the aubergine in plenty of salted water and set aside for an hour so they sweeten. Sauté the onion in the olive oil until lightly translucent.
2. Add the strained eggplants, shake the sauce pan and let it cook for 3-4 minutes. After add the tomato and 4 tbsp water. Cook uncovered only for 7 minutes.
3. Fill with 5 cups of water this time and when it starts boiling put the rice in, whisk well, cover and boil slowly for about 20 minutes.
4. Open the lid, turn off the heat, sprinkle with the mint, whisk gently, cover with a cloth towel and let the aubergine and rice to absorb its liquids for 10-12 minutes.

Serve this food with lots of freshly ground pepper and fresh mint

10. BUTTER BEANS IN THE OVEN

INGREDIENTS:

1 cup olive oil
2 cups butter beans
2 onions finely sliced
1 bunch parsley chopped
2 garlic cloves cut in thin rings
1 tsp tomato paste
1 large ripe tomato blended
1 medium tomato cut in thin slices
1 tsp oregano
½ tsp cumin
3-4 drops lemon juice
1 tsp sugar
salt, pepper.

METHOD:

1. Soak the beans overnight, for at least 8 hrs in plenty of cold water. Rinse thoroughly and boil in plenty of water for 25 minutes. Strain and set aside.
2. In a saucepan sauté the onion and the garlic for 3-4 minutes until translucent.
3. Add the celery, the tomato, the tomato paste dissolved in a cup of water, all the spices, the sugar and lemon juice. Mix well, add one more cup of water.
4. Cover the sauce andsimmer for 15-20 minutes. Arrange the butter beans in an oven proof dish or baking dish. Add the sauce over the beans.
5. Garnish with some tomato slices, sprinkle with a little salt and pepper and bake for 30-40 minutes in the oven, at 180º C. Serve hot, although it is tastier at room temperature.

11. ARTICHOKES WITH RICE

INGREDIENTS:

1 cup extra virgin olive oil with spicy taste
3 large heads of artichokes, cut in small pieces
2 fresh onions finely chopped
2 cups pilaf rice (not granular)
2 tbsp grated kefalotiri cheese or other hard cheese with a spicy taste
salt, fresh ground green pepper

METHOD:

1. Heat the oil and sauté the onions with the artichokes gently for about 10 minutes.
2. Add the salt and 7 cups of water. Let it boil, mix the rice and simmer for a further 20-25 minutes

uncovered.
3. When all the moisture is absorbed, mix again and remove the sauce pan from the heat. Cover it with a cotton kitchen towel and leave up to 10 minutes, until the mixture becomes moist.

Serve the dish hot with extra freshly ground pepper and sprinkle a small quantity of grated cheese on top.

12. STUFFED VEGETABLES

INGREDIENTS:

2 medium green peppers
2 medium ripe tomatoes
2 medium aubergine
2 medium courgettes
2 medium potatoes
2 medium artichokes
6 courgettes blossom flowers (optional)

FILLING

1 cup olive oil
1 cup tomato juice
200 gr rice
1 large onion roughly chopped
1 bunch parsley finely chopped
1 bunch dill finely chopped
1 bunch mint finely chopped
1 medium carrot, grated
2 sprigs of fresh onions
salt, pepper
1 tsp sugar

METHOD:

1. Wash and strain the vegetables well, make a round hole and hollow out their insides.
2. Cut the vegetable residue finely in a large bowl and keep aside. In the meantime sauté the onion with the olive oil, until translucent, add the herbs (parsley, dill, mint, fresh onions).
3. Peel, wash and grate the carrot, add it to the sauce pan with the other mixture. Add salt and pepper, according to taste.

4. Cook for 10 minutes with the tomato juice and the sugar, at a low temperature. Mix the contents of the vegetables without those of the potatoes, with the cooked herbs, for a further 10 minutes. Remove the mixture from the heat.

5. Wash and strain the rice in a strainer, incorporate well with the vegetable mixture. Lie the opened salted vegetables in a round or rectangular baking dish, fill up every one and close with their caps (the cut part from their top).

6. Pour around the rest of the strained mixture (only the liquids / not the solids). Sprinkle a pinch of grated hard cheese, or grated toast over every one of the stuffed vegetables. It is necessary to have nice presentation.

7. Bake in preheated oven at 180° C for 60 minutes, until golden on top.
Serve hot or warm, although the flavours are best at room temperature.

13. POTATO BALLS

INGREDIENTS

3 cups virgin olive oil
3 large very well boiled potatoes
1 cup of milk
3 eggs
2 large blended onions
3 tbsp butter
2 cups grated "kefalotiri cheese"(a kind of hard and spicy cheese)
1 cup parsley finely chopped
1 cup toast crumbs
1 tsp salt
½ tsp nutmeg
½ tsp pepper

METHOD:

1. Peel the cold boiled potatoes and blend in the electric grinder at a low speed or in the vegetable mill.

2. Sauté the onions gently with the butter until golden and they have absorbed their liquids.

3. Let them cool. Empty the mashed potatoes in a large bowl, make a hole in the middle and drop the eggs, the milk, the cheese, the onions, the butter, the parsley, the salt, the pepper

and the nutmeg in. Combine well by hand, to make a uniform mixture.

4. Whisk the mashed potatoes with the other ingredients, add the grated toast gradually, to make it more solid. Leave the mixture covered in the refrigerator, for 4-5 hours.

5. Heat the olive oil, at maximum heat in a small frying pan. Shape the round balls and place them one by one in the hot oil. Fry until golden around, strain the excess oil in kitchen paper and serve warm or cold at room temperature.

14. LONG GREEN PEPPERCORNS STUFFED WITH CHEESE PINK PEPPER AND SESAME

INGREDIENTS (for 8 people)

10 long sweet green peppers
1 cup sour soft cheese (mizithra, a kind of Cretan cheese)
1 cup sweet soft cheese (mizithra, the same kind of cheese but sweet)
1 tbsp pink pepper grains
1 tbsp white sesame
1 cup olive oil
salt

Greek cooking with olive oil makes it possible to have tasty vegetable dishes quickly.

METHOD:

1. Wash the peppercorns and let them dry slightly. Cut the top, from the stem, with a pointed knife, throw the seeds away and rinse the interior.

2. Put the pointed part of the peppercorns on the top of the strainer and leave them for at least 30 minutes, to drain completely.

3. In the meantime mix the cheese with a little salt in a bowl. Fill the peppercorns with this mixture.

4. Close, the peppercorns with it's lid and place them in a small oven proof bake dish next to each other.

5. Crush the pepper grains slightly in the mortar. Pour the olive oil on top, sprinkle the pepper and sesame on top.

6. Cook the peppercorns at 180 degrees for 40 minutes. The first twenty minutes cover them with aluminum foil.

Serve the peppercorns slightly warm, or at room temperature.

Summer Vegetables such as fresh beans, okra, aubergines and peppers are best cooked in olive oil as this keeps their flavour.

15. PEPPERCORNS WITH CHEESE BASIL OR MINT IN FORM

INGREDIENTS (for 10 people)

1 ½ kg sweet red peppercorns
½ kg soft feta cheese
4 tbsps sweet mizithra (Cretan soft cheese) or Filadelphia or cheese
2 tbsps basil or mint finely chopped
4 tbsps extra virgin olive oil
1 tsp vinegar
½ tsp green pepper
salt

METHOD:

1. Wash the peppercorns under cold running water. Arrange them on the grill in the oven and cook them for 20 minutes at 180 degrees.
2. In the meantime, chop the mint or basil finely in a small bowl, add 2 tbsps olive oil, the vinegar and the salt.
3. Whisk the mixture with a fork, so all the ingredients are combined well. Mix the cheeses in a second bowl, the rest of olive oil and the pepper until it becomes a similar mixture.
4. Take the peppercorns out of the oven and cover them with cling film, until they cool completely. Subtract the peel and seeds carefully.
5. Separating the peppercorns into two fillets. Drizzle both parts of the peppercorns slightly, with olive oil. Put some cling film on the bottom of a rectangular baking tray, so that it covers the sides, and it is essential for the cling film to be abundant on top and over the edge of the form.
6. On the bottom arrange some fillets of peppercorns, to covers the bottom completely.
7. Put some of the basil or mint on the top and right after, place the cheese mixture which is spread with a slightly oil spatula.
8. Continue in the same way placing each layer, alternately. Finish off, with a layer of peppercorns. The final thickness, must be approximately 6-7 cm. Put the baking tray in the fridge for 7-8 hours.
9. Take it out of the fridge, when you wish to serve. Remove the peppercorn dish and place it upside down on a serving plate. Remove the cling film carefully so, that you don't spoil the shape. Cut in thin slices with a sharp knife and serve accompanied with abundant green salad.

EGGS

1. FRIED EGGS WITH TOMATO SAUCE

INGREDIENTS

6 tbsp. extra virgin olive oil
1 large ripe tomato,
peeled and chopped
or grated
4 eggs
Salt
Pepper

METHOD

1. Heat a nonstick skillet.
   Add tomatoes , salt and simmer for 6 - 7 minutes, until all juices have evaporated.
2. Add olive oil.
   Stir and simmer for a further 2 - 3 minutes.
3. Break the eggs one by one over the tomatoes, taking care to keep the yolks intact. Occasionally spoon tomato sauce over eggs.
   Add pepper.
   Serve hot.

Eggs fried in olive oil and tomato sauce. Served with potatoes covered in olive oil and oregano.

2. OMELETTE WITH COURGETTES (ZUCCHINI SQUASH)

INGREDIENTS

3 medium courgettes, cut in fine rounds
6 eggs
2 tbsp. milk
1/3 cup (80 ml) extra virgin olive oil
1/2 tsp. salt
Freshly ground pepper

METHOD

1. Heat the oil in a nonstick skillet. Add the courgette rounds and fry on low until soft and light golden.

2. In the meantime whisk eggs, milk and salt , until frothy and yellowish.

3. Discard half of the frying oil and pour the egg mixture in the skillet.
    Fry for 2 - 3 minutes and turn the omelette.
    Fry for another 2 - 3 minutes on the other side.
    Repeat the turns once or twice, always on low heat , until the omelette is done in the centre and fried gently.

4. Serve the omelette hot and add the freshly ground pepper.

Zucchini omelette

3. OMELETTE WITH POTATOES

INGREDIENTS

1 cup olive oil
2 large potatoes cut in small cubes
6 eggs
salt, freshly ground pepper

METHOD

1. Heat the olive oil well, in a medium nonstick skillet.
2. Fry the potatoes for 20 minutes at a low temperature, covered.
3. In a bowl whisk the eggs with salt well. Remove the potatoes with a ladle and mix then into the bowl with the eggs.
4. Combine well and pour the egg mixture into a lightly oiled skilet.
5. Fry the omelette at a low temperature, for 7-8 minutes on one side and turn to the other, for another 7-8 minutes.
6. Repeat the turnovers once or twice, always at low heat, until the omelette is done in the centre.

Serve the omelette hot or at room temperature, and freshly grind a little pepper over it.

Fluffy omelette with potatoes

7

SPAGHETTI - MACARONI

SPAGHETTI WITH GARLIC AND OLIVE OIL

INGREDIENTS

1 cup olive oil
500 gr/1 lb spaghetti
6 garlic cloves, finely sliced
1 tsp salt
1 tsp freshly ground pepper

METHOD

1. Bring a large saucepan of salted water to the boil.
2. Add the pasta, stir and cook until al dente, (10-12 minutes).
3. Heat the oil in a saucepan, add the garlic and fry gently for 1-2 minutes until translucent.
4. Drain the spaghetti, add plenty of cold water, toss with the garlic mixture.
5. Season with black pepper and serve immediately in a large serving bowl.

SOUPS

1. FISH SOUP

INGREDIENTS

1/2 kilo (1 pound) cod fish
1/2 kilo red snapper
2 red mullets
2 large onions , quartered
2 large potatoes , quartered
1 cup (250 ml) extra virgin olive oil
1 tsp. salt
Juice of 1 lemon
Freshly ground pepper

METHOD

1. Clean and wash the fish under cold running water.
2. Heat the oil on low in a heavy bottomed skillet and sauté the onions. Line the potatoes over the onions and place the fish on top . Season. Fill with water to cover the fish.
3. Boil on high for 40 minutes , uncovered.
4. Remove from heat and add lemon juice.
5. Cover for 8 - 10 minutes and serve warm , with freshly ground pepper.

"Kakavia" is a famous fish, in which olive oil is an essential ingredient. It is very popular in Crete and in the Aegean.

2. LENTIL SOUP

INGREDIENTS

1/2 cup (125 ml) olive oil
2 1/2 cups lentils , medium size
2 cups of water
1 medium onion , finely chopped
2 garlic cloves , finely sliced
1 large carrot , cut in rounds
2 bay leaves
3 tbsp. balsamico vinegar ,or any strong flavored red wine vinegar
Salt
Pepper

METHOD

1. Pick and wash the lentils.
2. Heat oil on low temperature and sauté onions , garlic and lentils .
3. Add carrots , bay leaves , water, vinegar and spices. Season to taste and simmer for about 1 hour , until lentils are soft and the soup has thickened.

3. COLD SOUP WITH TOMATO YOGURT AND MINT

INGREDIENTS

1 tbsp extra virgin olive oil
4 large ripe tomatoes
1 cup onion finely chopped
1/3 of a big green pepper
1 piece of celery finely chopped
1 level tsp of sugar
1 level vinegar from red wine
2 tbsp yogurt
4 mint leaves finely chopped

METHOD

1. Dip the tomatoes for 1-2 minutes only in hot water. Remove with a slotted spoon and peel them.
2. Cut in quarters and squeeze with hands to remove the seeds. Cover the tomatoes and onions in a heavy bottomed skillet and sauté for 25 minutes.
3. Add the pepper, the celery and cook for a further 20 minutes.
4. According to taste add the sugar and the salt.
5. Remove from the heat and let the mixture cool for a little. Pulpify and transfer into a serving bowl. Keep the soup refrigerated for at least 2 hours.
6. Serve the soup cold in deep plates. On every plate add a tablespoon of fresh olive oil, thin out the yogurt with little water and put this mixture in a small bottle with a very narrow opening.
7. Shape different little designs with the thin paste, garnish with a pinch of mint and serve immediately.

4. MUSHROOM SOUP

INGREDIENTS

1 cup extra virgin olive oil
1 kg fresh mushrooms
2 sprigs fresh onions
1 small onion finely chopped
1 bunch of dill
1 egg
2 tbsp dry white wine
lemon juice
salt, green freshly ground pepper

METHOD

1. Clean and wash the mushrooms well, cut in small pieces and let them drain.
2. In a heavy bottomed skillet sauté the small onion, until all juices have evaporated, taking care not to burn.
3. Add the mushrooms, stir for 1-2 minutes.
4. Pour the wine in immediately adding 4 cups of water. Simmer covered for 20 minutes.
5. In the meantime prepare the dill and the onions sprigs mix well and continue to boil covered for a further 15 minutes. If necessary, add salt or pepper according to taste.
6. Wisk the egg until frothy preferably in a glass bowl. Add the lemon juice and warm broth from the soup gradually, beating continuously.
7. Pour this mixture into the pot and stir gently, to allow the sauce to thicken, season for 10 minutes and serve hot with a little fresh chopped dill and ground pepper.

FISH

1. FISH AND OKRA BAKED IN THE OVEN

INGREDIENTS

1 cup (250 ml) olive oil
4 - 5 fish fillets (bass, red snapper , haddock etc.)
1 kilo (2 pounds) okra
2 large onions , finely chopped
4 large ripe tomatoes (2 chopped finely , 2 sliced)
1 cup water
1/2 tsp. sugar
Juice of 1 large lemon
1 tbsp. vinegar
Salt
Pepper

METHOD

1.   Wash and dry fish. Arrange fillets in oven proof dish and season.
2.   Wash the okra and pour lemon juice on top . Set aside for 30 minutes.
3.   Arrange the okra around the fish, together with the juice from marinade.
4.   Mix together the tomato , onions , parsley , salt , pepper , oil and water.

Pour the mixture over the fish and vegetables.
5.   Bake in oven for 55 - 60 minutes at 180ºC /350ºF / Gas Mark 4.
Serve dish warm or at room temperature.

2. LEEKS AND SALTED COD RAGOUT

INGREDIENTS

3/4 cup (180 ml) olive oil
1 kilo (2 pounds) cod desalted and cut in pieces
1 kilo (2 pounds) leeks, cut in 5 cm long pieces
3/4 cup water
2 ripe tomatoes , cubed
2 tbsp. parsley, finely chopped
Salt
Pepper

METHOD

1. In a large heavy bottomed saucepan, heat oil and sauté the medium cut pieces of leeks gently, until golden.
2. Add a cup of water, salt and pepper, cover and simmer for 15 minutes.
3. Put the cod pieces gently on top of the leeks, sprinkle the chopped parsley and the sliced tomatoes.
4. Simmer for 25 minutes, covered.
   In the meantime shake the sauce several times carefully, without using with a fork. Serve warm or at room temperature.

Cod should be soaked in clean ,cold water for at least 12 hours. Water must be changed several times.

3. SQUIDS IN WINE , GREEN OLIVES AND DILL

INGREDIENTS

1 kilo (2 pounds) fresh squids , cleaned and cut in rings
3 /4 cup extra virgin olive oil
2 medium onions , finely chopped
1 spring onion , finely cut
1 1/2 cup dry white wine
1 cup water
1 1/2 cup green olives , rinsed well in warm water and pitted
1 pinch sugar
Salt
Freshly ground pepper

METHOD

1. Sauté onions in oil.
   Add squids and gently turn for 4 - 5 minutes until juices are evaporated , taking care not to burn.
2. Add wine , mix well and bring to a gentle boil .
3. Add a cup of water , sugar and season.
4. Add olives , spring onion and dill.
   Simmer for a further 35 - 40 minutes , uncovered.
   Serve either hot or at room temperature .

4. FISH WITH SAGE LEAVES SHRIMPS AND MUSSELS

INGREDIENTS

1 cup virgin olive oil
1 kg fish fillet (perch, red snapper)
1 cup of peeled shrimps
1 cup shelled mussels
1 tsp sage powder
3 large tomatoes finely chopped
½ cup dry white wine
½ cup toast crumbs
salt, freshly ground pepper

METHOD

1. Wash and strain the fish very well.
2. Arrange them in a round baking dish or in an oven proof dish with the mussels and the shrimps.
3. Salt gently, then mix the tomato with the sage, the olive oil, the wine and the rest of the salt and the pepper in a bowl.
4. Pour the mixture around the fish, shrimps and mussels with this mixture. Sprinkle on the toast crumbs and bake at 180º C for 50-55 minutes.
   Serve the fish either at room temperature or cold.

5. CUTTLEFISH WITH ITS INK

INGREDIENTS

1 ½ cup virgin olive oil
1 kilo small, fresh cuttlefishe
1 large onion grated
2 tbsp dry white wine
salt.

METHOD

1. Firstly clean the cuttlefish, taking out the spinal column (it is like a boat).
2. Pay attention to removing the intestine and its ink. Wash them under cold running water, cutting them in pieces if large. Keep out 3-4 bags full of ink.
3. Heat the olive oil and sauté the onion until the water is absorbed, being careful not to burn it.
4. Add the cuttlefish and sauté, gently turning, from side to side once or twice, until golden.
5. Add 2 cups of water, cover the pot with the lid and boil gently for 30 minutes.
6. Open the pot, add the ink, the salt and the wine. Mix well and continue boiling uncovered for 25-30 minutes, until the cuttlefish is done - that is when all the juices have evaporated and only its oil remains.

6. FISH BAKED IN GREASE PROOF PAPER

INGREDIENTS

5 tbsp extra virgin olive oil
1 large perch fillet
2 small garlic cloves, cut in thin slices
1 tsp rosemary
salt
fresh ground green pepper

METHOD

1. Wash and salt the fish.
2. Place the fish fillet in the centre of some greaseproof paper.
3. Sprinkle the garlic, the rosemary and the pepper on top.
4. Drizzle olive oil on top of the fish, fold the greaseproof paper and close tightly.
5. Bake at 200ºC for 45 minutes. Serve immediately with the remaining sauce.

7. FRIED RED - MULLETS

INGREDIENTS

2 cups virgin olive oil
1 kilo red-mullets medium size
1 ½ cup all purpose flour
1 level tbsp salt
10 leaves from a lemon tree

METHOD

1. Clean, wash and salt the red-mullet lightly. Strain and let them dry.
2. Mix the flour in a bowl with the rest of the salt. Flour them well. In the meantime heat the oil at a high temperature.
3. Shake the excess flour off the red-mullets and deep fry them in hot olive oil, uncovered.
4. Make sure each fish is under oil at all times, or turn continuously until they get a gold brown colour.
5. Place, the fish on double kitchen paper to absorb the excess oil.
   Cover a plate with lemon leaves and serve the red mullet.

8. CUTTLEFISH WITH BROAD BEANS, FENNEL, CRUSHED OLIVES AND SAUCE OF FLOUR AND LEMON JUICE.

INGREDIENTS

3 medium size cuttlefish, cleaned and cut in to small pieces
1 kilo green broad beans
1 cup of crushed olives or small green olives
1 cup of fennel finely chopped
4 spring onions finely sliced
1 cup of olive oil
1 tbsp flour juice of a large fresh lemon
salt, pepper

METHOD

1. In a pot sauté the cuttlefish with the olive oil until all the juices have evaporated.
2. Add 2 cups of water, cover and let them boil gently for 35-40 minutes.
3. Try with a fork to see if they are soft. Then add the spring onions, the fennel, the pepper a little salt, the broad beans cleaned and cut in half (if large).
4. When it absorbs its fluids add some water and boil for 20 minutes, covered. When the cuttlefish and broad beans are cooked , put in the olives and stir gently

with a spoon.

5. Remove from heat after 6-8 minutes and add the flour that has been dissolved to the lemon juice. Let it stand for 10 minutes before serving.

9. "FIRE SHRIMPS" WITH CHEESE

INGREDIENTS

24 big shrimps,
6 peeled ripe and tomatoes
1 onion, crushed
1 cup extra virgin olive oil
1 tbsp vinegar
1 tbsp sugar
salt, coarsely ground pepper
150 gr feta cheese, grated

METHOD

1. Boil the shrimps in plenty salted water only for 3 minutes.

2. Strain the shrimps with slotted spoon and let dry and cool. Remove the shells by holding the head and the tail.

3. Pay attention to removing the intestine. In the meantime prepare the sauce separately.

3. Fry onions until translucent, saute the finely chopped tomatoes.
   Add the tbsp of sugar and vinegar.

5. Add the salt and roughly ground pepper. Simmer until all juices have evaporated.
   Arrange the shrimps in an oven proof dish. Drizzle the sauce over the shrimps.

6. Sprinkle cheese on top. Leave for a further 10 minutes uncovered and grill, until golden and serve.

10. STUFFED SQUIDS

INGREDIENTS:

12 medium sized squid
360 gr feta cheese
2 small onions finely sliced
200 gr tomato paste
5 tsp parsley finely chopped
2 glasses white wine
salt, pepper, paprika
One of my oldest and best recipes.

METHOD

1. Firstly clean and wash the squid under cold running water, cutting off the head.
2. Take the spinal column, and the tentacles off the body. Chop the tentacles to add to the filling.
3. In a large bowl mix the cheese with the tomato paste and add all the ingredients, except for the wine.
4. Fill the squids with the filling and fold them with a tooth – pick. Mix the rest of the filling with the wine. Put the squids in a baking dish and cover with the rest of the filling.
5. Bake at 200ºC for 1 hour. Let them cool for a while, then cut

them in fat rings and serve with snow white rice.

11. BAKED FISH WITH FRESH TOMATO SAUCE AND OLIVE OIL

INGREDIENTS:

1 cup (exceptional) virgin olive oil
4-5 slices (gurnard fish, pike fish, or tuna fish)
2 medium ripe tomatoes finely chopped
1 tbsp parsley finely chopped
3 drops lemon juice
salt, pepper

METHOD

1. Wash, salt and roast, bake or grill the fish.
2. Mix the tomato with the olive oil well in a bowl. Add the parsley, the lemon juice, the salt and the pepper.
3. Pour the tomato sauce and olive oil over the fish and serve.

MEAT AND POULTRY

1. ROAST BEEF WITH EGGPLANTS (AUBERGINES)

INGREDIENTS

1 cup (250 ml) olive oil
1 kilo (2 pounds) eggplants
2 garlic cloves , finely sliced
1 kilo beef , cubed
2 large onions , roughly chopped
1 tbsp. parsley , finely minced
2 large ripe tomatoes , cubed
1 cup broth
1/2 cup water   (a little more if needed)
1 tsp. lemon juice
Salt
Pepper

METHOD

1. Wash the aubergine and cut lengthwise into pieces which are 3-4 cm thick. Soak in salted cold water for 50 minutes.
2. In the meantime, bring the beef to the boil and cook on high heat for 35 minutes. Save 1 cup of broth.
3. Strain eggplants, Arrange beef and eggplants in an oven proof dish .
4. Mix tomatoes, onions, parsley, lemon juice and saved beef broth. Add the mixture over the beef and eggplants.
5. Drizzle oil and 1/2 cup water over the top. Bake covered for 20 minutes in a hot oven .
   Lower the temperature and bake for a further hour .
   Turn the oven off and leave for a further 20 minutes uncovered.

Serve warm , although the flavours are best at room temperature.

Roast veal with aubergines

2. PORK WITH CELERY - EGG AND LEMON SAUCE

INGREDIENTS

1 kilo (2 pounds) pork shoulder, cut in portions
2 onions , finely sliced
2 large celery roots, cut in large cubes
1 large celery stick , cut in 4 - 5 cm. (1 1/4 - 1 3/4 inch) pieces
3 - 4 cups of water
2 eggs ,beaten
1 cup (250 ml) extra virgin olive oil
3/4 cup (180 ml) dry white wine
Juice of 1 lemon
1 tsp. salt
1/2 tsp. ground pepper

METHOD

1. Heat the oil and sauté the onions , until translucent.
2. Wash and dry the portions of pork. Add them to the onions . Turn once or twice until golden.
3. Add wine , one cup of water and simmer covered , for 20 minutes .
4. Add celery and 2 - 3 cups of water . Season .
5. Add pepper and simmer covered , for 45 - 50 minutes .
6. Finish off cooking with the temperature switched off.
7. In the meantime prepare the egg and lemon sauce. Whisk eggs until frothy. Add the lemon juice gradually and warm broth from the pork , beating continuously, until the sauce is as hot as the juices of pork in the pot.
8. Pour the lemon and egg sauce in the pot and shake it gently , to allow sauce to mingle with pork and vegetables.
9. Serve hot .

3. LAMB MARINATED IN OLIVE OIL, VINEGAR AND ONION

INGREDIENTS

1 medium size lamb thigh without bones, cut in small cubes
6 pita breads
3 tbsp strained yogurt
2 tbsp parsley finely chopped
1 medium size tomato, cut in cubes

For the marinade sauce:
½ cup olive oil
1 large onion finely sliced
1 tsp salt
1 tbsp vinegar from red wine
½ tsp thyme
1 tsp black pepper

Preparation of the marinade sauce:

Empty the olive oil in a clay bowl and squeeze the onion with hands to remove excess liquids.

METHOD

1. Add the salt, the vinegar, the thyme, the pepper and the lamb, and leave for 12 hours.
2. Drain the lamb from the marinade, put the pieces to grill or roast on a spit, salt according to taste.
3. Serve the lamb pieces over or inside the pita bread with a small quantity of yogurt, parsley and tomato.

4. PORK WITH RICE AND CARDAMOME

INGREDIENTS

½ cup extra virgin olive oil
1 tbsp fresh butter
1 ½ kg pork shoulder, cut in small pieces
½ kg long rice,
1 cup vermicelli
1 big onion finely chopped
7-8 grams green cardamome
salt, freshly ground green pepper

METHOD

1. Fill up a skillet with water, and "blue" the meat for 2-3 minutes.
2. Empty the skillet and change the water, sprinkle the salt, the onion and little pepper. Boil for 50-60 minutes.
3. Strain the pork meat and keep aside 6 cups of broth.

In a large - deep frying pan heat the cardamome, when they start to crack and release their aroma, add the rice and sauté for 5-6 minutes whisking continuously.

4. Drop in the broth and lower the heat. Place in the meat, whisk using a spoon, and set the rice to simmer for 10 minutes. Turn off the heat and leave covered with a cotton towel, for the rice to swell.
5. In a small frying pan heat the butter, drop in the vermicelli paste and cook until translucent, taking care not to burn it.
6. Strain the vermicelli and put it together with the meat and the rice. Whisk well and sprinkle lots of freshly ground pepper on top. Serve immediately.

5. FRIED PORK WITH CORIANDER

INGREDIENTS

1 cup extra virgin olive oil
1 kg pork shoulder, cut in small cubes
1 tsp crushed coriander
½ tsp green pepper
1 tsp salt not full
juice of 1 lemon

METHOD

1. Wash the pork meat well and put it into a heavy deep pot with a lid, without straining.
2. Simmer with its liquids at medium heat and cover for about 20 minutes. When the liquids are absorbed, add one cup of water, cover and simmer again for 25-30 minutes.
3. Add the coriander, season with salt, pepper and the oil. Fry gently until golden from all sides and stir 2-3 times, so the pork gets the aroma of the spices.
4. Finish off cooking with the cooker turned off but don't remove from the heat, add plenty of drops of lemon juice over the meat.
5. Place the used lemon face down over the pork meat, cover and let it stand for 7-9 minutes. Serve hot with the sauce.

It could be accompanied with fried potatoes and green salad.

6. LAMB STEW

INGREDIENTS

4-5 cup virgin olive oil
1 ½ kg lamb shoulder, cut in small pieces
salt

METHOD

1. Wash the meat well and leave aside to strain.
2. Salt and transfer into a heavy bottomed skillet, add the olive oil to cover the portions of lamb, make sure that the meat is completely covered.
3. Cook covered at maximum heat for 5-8 minutes. Open the lid, add a cup of water and continue cooking the lamb at the same temperature for at least 45-50 minutes.
4. Remove the meat with a slotted ladle and serve hot with its sauce.

7. OILY CAULIFLOWER WITH PORK

INGREDIENTS

1 cup virgin olive oil
1 large cauliflower cut in medium sized pieces
1 kilo pork shoulder cut in small pieces
2 tbsp parsley finely chopped
1 ½ large tomato cut in small cubes
1 large onion finely sliced, salt, pepper.

METHOD

1. Heat the oil at a low temperature in a heavy – bottomed skillet and sauté the onions for 3-4 minutes.
2. Add the pork and let it sauté until slightly golden. Add 2 cups of water, lower the temperature, cover and boil slowly for about 30 minutes.
3. Uncover the skillet, with a fork "pinch" the meat. If it is almost done, add the parsley, the salt and the pepper.
4. Remove the meat with a large spoon and make place to put the cauliflower florets on top.
5. Add the tomato and the salt and cover. Continue cooking for another 20 minutes.
6. With a ladle, stir well being careful to keep the cauliflower intact. Continue boiling at a moderate temperature for 15-20 minutes, uncovered. Serve warm or cold at room temperature, with freshly ground pepper.

8. SMALL COURGETTE, KID GOAT AND OLIVE OIL

INGREDIENTS

3 cups of olive oil for frying
10 small courgette
3 garlic cloves, finely sliced
2 ripe tomatoes, cubed
2 large potatoes coarsely chopped for frying
1 kilo (2 pounds) kid goat cut in small portions
1 large onion, coarsely chopped
½ tea spoon sugar, salt, pepper.

METHOD

1. Wash the courgette very well. Make a cut in them, lengthwise from one side only, in every opening put a slice of garlic.
2. Heat a nonstick skillet with a cup of oil and fry the courgette gently for 7-8 minutes, turn over once or twice, being careful not to burn.
3. Strain, on kitchen paper and continue, adding one more cup oil to fry the potatoes.
4. Drain them on kitchen paper too. Heat the 3rd cup of oil in a large heavy – bottom skillet and sauté the onion for 3-4 minutes.
5. Arrange the meat and let it sauté gently. Fill with 2 cups of water and simmer for 30 minutes.
6. Try with a fork to see if the meat is done. If it is almost ready, mix the tomato with sugar, salt and pepper. After that, arrange the meat with a spoon among the fried potatoes and courgette.
7. Put the tomato sauce on top, cover and simmer for 20-25 minutes.
8. Finish off cooking with the heat turned off, uncovered. Serve hot or at room temperature.

Small courgette with tenter kid goat and olive oil sauce

9. KID GOAT WITH OIL AND OREGANO

INGREDIENTS

1 cup of virgin olive oil
1 leg of kid goat about 1 ½ kg
1 cup dry white wine
1 soup spoon oregano
1 soup spoon flour
1 tea spoon salt, pepper, lemon juice

METHOD

1. Cut the meat in portions, wash without straining and put into the pot. Simmer covered until all the water has evaporated
2. Add olive oil, mix thoroughly and sauté gently, drizzle wine on top and stir.
3. Dissolve the flour in 1 ½ cup of water and add it to the pot with the oregano, salt, pepper and lemon.
4. Simmer for 30-35 minutes covered.

Serve with its sauce and fried potatoes.

10. MEAT BALLS

INGREDIENTS

2 cups olive oil
½ kilo minced beef
½ kilo minced lamb
6 large finely chopped onions
1 crushed garlic glove
1 egg
2 more tbsp olive oil
1 cup all purpose flour
1 tsp oregano
1 tsp pepper
½ tsp cumin
1 tsp salt

METHOD

1. Place the minced meat in a bowl and make an opening in the centre.
2. In there put the onion, the egg, the cumin, the oregano, the salt and the garlic. Combine well with your hands in circular movements, until completely blended.
3. Place the mixture in the refrigerator for 3-4 hrs, until the spices are well combined.
4. Take the mixture out of the fridge, add the olive oil and knead again for 2-3 minutes.
5. In a heavy-bottomed skillet, heat the oil to a high temperature. Shape with hands into small balls, flour them and, deep fry them in the hot oil.
6. Fry and turn them around until they get a golden brown colour.
7. Place each meat ball on kitchen paper to absorb excess oil and continue frying until all the meat balls are used.

11. "PASTITSIO"

FOR THE BESAMEL CREAM

2 tbsp corn flour
3 tbsp olive oil
1 bottle of warm milk
salt, pepper, nutmeg powder
1 egg (optional)

FOR THE FILLING "MINCED MEAT"

1 kg minced beef
2 onions finely chopped
1 white wine glass
2 cups tomato juice
salt, pepper, powder of cinnamon
½ kg slotted spaghetti
butter to saute
½ kg kind of graviera

METHOD

1. Boil the spaghetti in plenty of salted water for 6-8 minutes. In the meantime, prepare the minced meat. Heat the oil in a large saucepan, add onions mix the minced meat thoroughly and sauté the ingretients until combined and cook slowly with wine.

2. Add the tomato juice and spices and bring to a slow boil, until soft.

3. Remove from heat when the water is absorbed.

4. Now prepare the besamel cream. In a large heavy saucepan, heat the butter and corn flour gently.

5. Gradually add warm milk until well combined.
Let it stand for a few minutes to cool off and whisk the egg by beating continuously.

6. Mix the salt, pepper and nutmeg powder, with 1/5 of cheese and add the eggs.

7. Stir well. Transfer the spaghetti, the mince meat and sauce and the rest of the cheese into a lightly oiled oven proof dish.
Stir all those ingredients well.

8. Spread these ingredients and cover with the besamel cream.

9. Trim the surface of cream with a knife and bake in preheated oven for 1 hour at 180ºC.

12." GIOULBASI "

INGREDIENTS

½ kilo lamb cut in portions
½ kilo pork cut in portions
½ kilo beef cut in portions
½ kilo graviera cubed
3 onions cut in fine rings
4 garlic cloves
½ cup fresh butter
½ olive oil
3 tbsp black pepper
salt
5-6 sheets grease - proof paper

METHOD

1. In a large bowl mix all the kinds of meat onions and garlic. Add the salt, pepper and the cheese, mixing all the ingredients well, then add the butter.

2. Spread out one sheet of grease – proof paper and put the meat in the center, fold up like an envelope.

3. Spread out the second sheet put the first package in the centre, but this time the opening must face downwards, folding it up in to an envelope again.

4. Continue this procedure until 4-5 sheets have been used.

5. Attention the last sheet must have the opening upwards so as not to lose all the meat's juices.

6. Finally tie the package well with a string. Bake in the oven until soft (approx. 2 or 3 hours). When opening the package a delicate fragrance will released.

Meat which has been marinated in olive oil becomes softer. So game, beef and pork are best with olive oil

11

PIES - BISCUITS - CAKES

1.SPINACH PIE

INGREDIENTS

FOR THE FILLING

1 kilo (2 pounds) fresh spinach, roughly chopped
1 bunch parsley , finely minced
1 bunch fresh mint , finely minced
7 - 8 spring onions , finely sliced
1 kilo (2 pounds) feta cheese , mashed with fork or grated if hard
2 eggs , beaten
1 tsp. pepper
1 tsp. powder nutmeg
1/2 tsp. salt (careful if feta cheese is salty)

FOR THE FILO PASTRY

1 packet (1/2 kilo / 1 pound) store bought filo pastry
4 tbsp. extra virgin olive oil

METHOD

1. Place spinach and aromatic herbs in a large bowl. Season. Squeese with hands to remove excess liquids. Drain.
2. Add feta cheese , beaten eggs and spices .
3. Brush a 30 cm. (11 1/2 inch) diameter high baking dish with oil.
4. Divide filo sheets in to parts. Line one sheet flat in the bottom of the baking dish. Make sure the filo covers the sides of the baking tray aswell. Repeat until 4 - 5 sheets are used , brushing each one as it is added.
5. Add the filling.

Every kind of pie or pastry contains generous amounts of olive oil which provides a different and delicious taste. Try using olive oil in your dough for pizza, pancakes and flat bread and your dough for pizza, pancakes and flat bread and you will be enchanted by the result!

6. Trim the edges of the pastry, stricking out around the dish with a sharp knife.
7. Cover with the rest of the filo sheets , brushing each one with oil. Cut the pastry in diagonal parallel lines , about 4 cm. (1 /13 inch) apart and then cut them across to form diamond shapes.
8. Bake in preheated oven at
    180 C - 350F - Gas Mark 4 for 50 - 60 minutes.
9. Serve warm or at room temperature.

2. KALITSOUNIA

(Small , half moon shaped, fried pies, stuffed with soft white cheese and mint)

INGREDIENTS

FOR THE DOUGH

1/2 cup extra virgin olive oil
2 cups all purpose flower
3 - 4 drops of lemon juice
1/2 tsp. salt
3/4 cup lukewarm water
2 cups olive oil for frying
Sugar to sprinkle

FOR THE FILLING

3 cups soft white cheese , cut in small cubes
1 tsp. fresh mint , finely minced
1 egg yolk
1 tbsp. sugar
1/2 tsp. powder cinnamon

DOUGH METHOD

1. Mix flour , lemon juice , oil and warm water , in a mixer bowl at medium speed for approximatly 4 minutes , until well combined to a soft mixture . Add water or flour if needed.
2. Place dough on floured surface, covered with a cloth for 10 minutes .

FILLING

3. Mix cheese , mint , sugar , cinnamon and egg yolk together .
4. Divide dough in half
5. Roll out to about 1/2 cm. thick. Cut some circles of 5 - 6 cm. diameter each.
6. Place 1 tsp. of filling in the middle . Fold over to half moon shape and press edges together , making sure they are completely closed.
7. Deep fry in hot oil . Serve immediately , sprinkled with sugar.

Olive oil gives a special taste when we use it as an ingredient and also makes the bread crust crunchy and golden. The olive oil prevents the bread from sticking to the baking tin.

3. DEEP FRIED PIES

INGREDIENTS

500 gr. all purpose flour
5 tbsp. extra virgin olive oil
Juice of one large orange
4 tbsp. grappa or vodka
1/2 tsp. salt
1/2 tsp. powder cinnamon
2 cups lukewarm water (and a little more if needed)
1 1/2 cup olive oil for frying
Honey or sugar (according to taste) for topping

METHOD

1. Place flour in a large bowl and make a well in the centre.
2. Add oil, orange juice, grappa or vodka salt and cinnamon. Mix together and knead for 5 minutes, adding a little warm water to avoid sticking , until dough is soft and ready to cut.
3. Cut dough in to pieces the size of a small orange.
4. Roll out each piece into circles of approx. 1cm. thick and 13-15 cm diameter.
5. Deep fry the pies making sure each pie is under oil at all times, pressing with a fork if necessary.
6. Remove the pies from the oil once they have risen and taken a gold brown colour.
7. Place each pie on kitchen paper to absorb excess oil and continue to fry until all pies are used.

Serve warm with honey or sugar according to taste .

Deep fried pies. This recipe is extremely simple and the dough deep fried in olive oil becomes deliciously crunchy.

4. BISCUITS WITH OLIVE OIL

INGREDIENTS

1 cup olive oil
1 kilo all purpose flour
2 cups sugar
1 cup fresh orange juice
1 cup dry red wine
1 tsp. baking powder
1 tbsp. honey
1 tsp powder cinnamon
1/2 tsp. aniseed , crushed
1 cup walnuts , coarsely crushed

METHOD

1. In a medium saucepan warm the wine on low heat and dissolve the sugar and honey. Add orange juice, olive oil, cinnamon, aniseed and walnuts.
2. Mix well and remove from heat. Do not boil.
3. Mix together the flour and baking powder and add gradually to the saucepan . Combine well. Shape with hands into small rounds and place on oiled cooking tray.
4. Bake in preheated oven for 40 minutes at 11OC - 225F - Gas Mark 1/4 .
5. Remove from oven and sprinkle with sugar . Cool. Keep in a cool place in an airtight tin.

Biscuits with lots of olive oil and spices.

5. RAISIN CAKE

INGREDIENTS

1 1/2 cup (375 ml) extra virgin olive oil
1 kilo (2 pounds) plain flour
2 cups sugar
1 1/2 cup lukewarm water
1/2 cup (125 ml) brandy
1 cup fresh orange juice
2 1/2 cups raisins , cut in half
1 tbsp. powder nutmeg
1 tsp. cloves
A pinch of cinnamon
1 tsp. baking soda , dissolved in the orange juice
1 tsp. baking powder

METHOD

1. In a large bowl, mix the sugar, and olive oil, with your hands in circular movements until completely blended.
2. Add water , brandy , spices , and soda dissolved in

orange juice.

3. Mix flour and baking powder. Add gradually to the bowl and mix well until the dough is thick .

4. Transfer mixture to a lightly oiled oven proof dish , drizzle a little oil on top and bake for 45 - 60 minutes at 180 C - 350F- Gas Mark 4. To check readiness , pierce centre of cake (it should come out clean).

5. Cool and cut the cake in squares.

Cake with raisins and olive oil.
Try replacing butter with olive oil in all cakes muffins and brownies.

6. BAKLAVA

INGREDIENTS

1packet (1/2 kilo) store bought filo pastry
3 1/2 cups walnuts , coarsely crushed
1 1/2 cup extra virgin olive oil
2 tbsp. honey
2 tbsp. sugar
1 tbsp. powder cinnamon
20 cloves (optional)*

METHOD

1. Mix the walnuts , sugar and cinnamon in a bowl.

2. Brush the bottom of a round or rectangular baking dish with oil. Lie in one piece of filo pastry and fold it up on the sides. Repeat with the other 3 sheets , brushing with oil as each one is added.

3. Place the walnut mixture on top.

4. Trim the edges of the sheets which are sticking out around the dish with a sharp knife.

5. Cover with the rest of the filo sheets, brushing each one .

6. Cut the top sheets with diagonal parallel lines, about 4 cm. (1 1/3 inch) apart and then across to form medium size diamond shapes.

7. Bake at 180 C - 350F - Gas

Mark 4 for 50 minutes , until golden.

8. Remove from the oven and while still hot, pure honey on top.

Optional* Stud one clove on each piece of baklava.

"Baklavas" this classical Greek dessert becomes wonderfully light when extra virgin olive oil is used instead of butter. This dessert can also be stuffed with almonds or dried fruit.

7. BAKE ROLLS WITH BUTTER AND OLIVE OIL

INGREDIENTS

2 ½ cups olive oil
1 ½ cup butter
3 cups sugar
1 ½ cup fresh orange juice
1 egg
1 tsp soda
1 ½ tsp baking powder
1 ½ kg white flour
(approximately)

METHOD

1. In a plastic or glass bowl mix the butter at full speed and then the olive oil and the sugar by hand, until all the ingredients are combined well.

2. Dissolve the soda, into the orange juice and mix the baking powder with the flour. Add the egg to this mixture and add that then to the first.

3. Knead the dough adding the rest of the flour gradually until it becomes soft. Combine well, shaping with hands into small rolls and place on an oiled cooking tray.

4. Bake in the middle of the oven for about 45 minutes, until golden.

8. BISCUITS WITH VODKA OR RAKI

INGREDIENTS

1 ½ cup virgin olive oil
1 ½ cup sugar
2 pieces mastic powder
1 kg and 1 more cup of flour
1 cup vodka or raki
2-3 tbsp sugar
juice of two large lemons

METHOD

1. In a large bowl empty the olive oil and mix with the sugar until it froths lightly.
2. Incorporate the lemon juice with the other mixture and the mastic powder.
3. Add the flour gradually and knead with the vodka or raki. When the dough becomes hard enough, shape with hands into small rolls and place on an oiled small baking dish. Sprinkle the sugar on top and bake at 180ºC for 50-60 minutes.

9. PIE WITH DRIED FIGS AND ALMONDS

INGREDIENTS

1 cup extra virgin olive oil
10 dried figs chopped
3 cups all purpose flour
2-2 ½ cups self raising flour
1 cup almonds finely crushed
1 tbsp coarsely crushed almonds
1 tbsp grated orange peel
½ cup sugar
½ cup honey
1 cup fresh orange juice
2 eggs
1 ½ tsp baking powder
½ tsp salt
½ tsp cinnamon powder
1-2 crushed cloves

METHOD

1. Sprinkle the figs with 2 tbsp flour.
2. Empty the olive oil in a bowl with the sugar and the honey and whisk lightly, until whitened. Add the eggs and continue blending with the electrical blender, until well combined with the rest of the mixture.
3. Lastly add the orange juice.
4. In a second clean bowl, mix the flour, the cinnamon, the baking powder, the cloves, the salt and the finely crushed almonds.
5. Mix the second mixture with the solids in the first bowl with the liquids and work fast for 5-6 minutes, until it turns into a thick mixture like a cream.
6. Add the floured figs and the peel of the orange and stir again with a ladle or another suitable gadget to combine all the quantity into the mixture.
7. Brush a 36 cm diameter high baking dish, lightly with oil and transfer the mixture. Sprinkle with coarsely around almonds and bake in preheated oven for 50-60 minutes at 180º C.

10. FRIED SWEET MOUTH FULLS

INGREDIENTS

FOR THE CRUST

1 cup warm water
1 tbsp virgin olive oil
1 tbsp red wine
1 egg, separate the yolk from the white
4 tbsp milk
½ packet baking powder
4-5 tbsp hard flour
6-7 cups common virgin olive oil for frying
fine sugar or honey

FOR THE FILLING
½ kg strained misithra (sweet, soft cheese,like the Italian ricotta)
1 tsp powder cinnamon
2 tbsp sugar

METHOD

1. Drop the warm water, the olive oil, the red wine, the milk and the egg yolk into a bowl.
2. Whisk the mixture with a fork. Incorporate the baking powder with the flour and drop the rest of the mixture. Stir again with the fork until it turns into a thin paste, let it stand for 2 hours in the fridge .
3. In the mean time, stir the misithra with the cinnamon and the sugar. Combine well.
4. Shape with hands into smaller than nut size balls. Keep refrigerated for 2 hours.Take the paste from the fridge, whisk the white of the egg until frothy and incorporate with the paste.
5. Stir gently with a fork. Heat the olive oil until it is very hot, dip the small balls of the misithra into the paste and place into the oil immediately, making sure each ball is covered in oil at all times.
6. When it forms a golden brown crust, transfer from the oil onto kitchen towel, then into a bowl.

Serve with plenty of honey or sprinkle fine sugar over the top.

Crunchy, spicy cookie with olive oil, cinnamon and cummin

11. HALVA

INGREDIENTS

1 ½ cup common virgin olive oil
1 package fine flour
1 cup all purpose flour
For the syrup
3 cups sugar
6 cups water
1 tsp grated lemon peel
powdered cinnamon

METHOD

1. Heat the olive oil in a heavy bottomed skillet and let it smoke. Gradually add fine flour, mixing fast and continuously with a wooden ladle until it becomes brown.
2. After this, add the flour and whisk well together.
3. Prepare the syrup, dissolve the sugar into six glasses of hot water. Take care to dissolve it completely and add the grated lemon.
4. When the fine flour cooks enough and takes a golden brown colour, pour in the syrup gradually and stir continuously so it doesn't over flow.
5. The moment that the fine flour absorbs the syrup completely, remove the skillet from the heat and cover with a cotton towel for about 10 minutes.
6. Take spoonfuls and arrange on a serving dish, or better, over lemon leaves or bitter orange leaves. Sprinkle with a pinch of cinnamon powder and serve.

12. CAKE WITH OLIVE OIL

INGREDIENTS

5 cups virgin olive oil
2 cups orange juice
3 ½ cups sugar
1 tbsp soda, half full
1 tsp powder of cinnamon
2 pieces crushed mastic
5 crushed cloves
6-7 cups white flour
2 tbsp sesame

METHOD

1. In a bowl whisk the olive oil with the sugar until lightly froths.
2. Dissolve the soda into the orange juice and add this mixture to the other with the olive oil. Incorporate the cinnamon powder and the mastic powder with the cloves.
3. Knead for 1-2 minutes to mix the ingredients well.
4. Start to drop the flour in gradually, mixing continuously, until the mixture becomes thickened.
5. Brush the bottom of an oven proof dish lightly with oil and transfer the mixture there. Sprinkle abundantly with sesame and bake at 180º C for 50-60 minutes.

13. HONEY – PIE

INGREDIENTS

2 tea cups of olive oil
2 1/2 tea cups of thyme honey
1 tea cup of soup (broth) made from boiled cinnamon and cloves
1 tea cup of lemon juice
1 tea lemon rind
½ tea spoon of nutmeg
3 soup spoons of vodka or tsipouro
1 tea spoon of soda
1 tb baking powder
½ tea spoon of ground clove
1 tea cup of ground walnuts
770 grams of white flour
1 soup spoon of white sesame

PREPARATION

1. Mix the olive oil with the honey in the mixer for 3min.
    Melt the soda into the lemon juice and add all the fluids and spices.
2. Mix for 1min. so that all the ingredients are well combined. Blend the baking powder with the flour and gradually add the mixture which is in the mixer bowl.
3. Blend the mixture for another 5 min. at a moderate speed. The dough should be like thick

pulp. If more fluids are required, add some more lemon juice or some more raki or vodka (not water).

4. Add the walnuts and mix them nicely with a small wooden ladle, so that it becomes thick.

5. Empty the mixture into an oiled (size no 36). Sprinkle the mixture with sesame and cook in the oven at 180ºC for 60 min. approximately.

14. BOUREKI

(FROM CHANIA)

INGREDIENTS

1½ kilo green zucchini or pumpkin
4 potatoes
1 kilo of cottage cheese and half
1 kilo of shredded feta cheese
1 cup of creme
3 chopped tomatoes,
chopped mint, salt, pepper,
1 cup flour and a little olive oil.

Instructions:

1. Slice up the zucchini or pumpkin and the potatoes into very thin slices.

2. Put them in a large bowl with the chopped tomatoes, the mint half of the cheese, a little oil and 1½ cup of flour.

3. Mix them well and spread them on an oiled baking tray. Spread the rest of the cheese over these ingredients and put as much flour needed to cover it all.

4. Press the mixture with your hands so it becomes flat and pour the cream on top.

5. Bake it at high temperature for an hour and then cover it with foil and bake for another hour at medium temperature.

15. EASTER MEAT PIE

INGREDIENTS

FOR THE PASTRY
1½ Flour,
½ teaspoon yeast
1 cup of yogurt
1½ cup olive oil
Salt
as much warm water as needed to become a soft dough (approx 1 cup).

INGREDIENTS FOR FILLING
2 kilo lamb meat in cubes
1 kilo of ricota cheese,
1 kilo cottage cheese,
1 cup of cream
1 tsp fresh mint finelly chopped,
salt,
pepper.

INSTRUCTIONS

1. Prepare the pastry, divide into two parts and flatten them into thick pastry sheets and lay one pastry sheet onto the oily baking tray.
2. Prepare the meat, wash it and then let it drain. Add salt and pepper, put a layer of "ricota" cheese mixed with the cottage cheese.
3. Add two or three table spoons of cream.
4. After this lay the meat over the cheese and cover with the other pastry sheet.
5. Beat an egg, add some oil with the egg and then spread this mixture over the top of the pastry sheet.
6. Sprinkle sesame on top and bake it at medium temperature for two hours.

When the first hour passes, cover the pie with foil.

16. MILK- PIE

INGREDIENTS

1½ cups of fine flour
1 lt milk
1 ½ cup of sugar
2 soup spoons butter
2 soup spoons olive oil for the filo dough pastry
4 whisked eggs
2 vanilla

fine sugar
cinnamon powder

METHOD

1. Empty half of the fine flour into a large bowl. Mix the sugar, vanilla and whisked eggs together in circular movements with your hands.
2. Simmer the milk and add the warm milk gradually, in to the mixture. Combine well beating continuously.
3. Transfer the mixture and heat it in

a nonstick skillet and keep on stirring well. Add the butter gradually and the rest of the fine flour, stirring the mixture and be careful so that it doesn't boil. Let it cool.

4. Cut the filo pastry in lengthways pieces, about 15 cm.x 22 cm. Take the sheets and brush them well with butter. With a spoon put the filling on top of the sheet, turn the sheet around and roll it to form a rectangular shape.

5. Brush the bottom of a round or rectangular baking dish with olive oil. Put in the filo pastry. Repeat the brushing on the surface of each one. Bake at 180º C for about 45 minutes, until golden.

6. Remove from the oven and while still hot, sprinkle with fine sugar and cinnamon powder. (optional).

17. SMALL ONION PIES

INGREDIENTS

2 cups chopped onions in small chunks
½ cup chopped mint
½ cups fennel finely chopped
1 cup spinach, ½ cup flour
½ cup olive oil
salt, pepper
Pastry: juice from a lemon and an orange 1 tsp yeast, 1tbsp raki or vodka
1 ½ cups plain flour
1 tbsp olive oil
salt.

METHOD

1. Dissolve the yeast powder in in water, add the fluids the raki and the salt, lastly add the fluids the raki and the salt, lastly add the flour and make a thin pastry sheet and we cut out square or circular pieces of pastry sheet.

2. Put the filling ingredients into a bowl and mix with your hands. Stain the mixture and add the oil and flour so the mixture sticks together.

3. Put the filling onto the circular pieces of pastry.

4. Close the pastry and press them so the air comes out.

5. Bake them at low temperature. For 45 min until golden.

18. BISCUITS WITH OLIVE OIL AND CUMIN

INGREDIENTS

1 ½ cup olive oil
1 kilo wholemeal barley flour
½ kilo white flour
25 gr yeast
1 cup sugar
½ cup "raki" or "tsipouro"
1 cup fresh orange juice
1 tsp full freshly ground cumin

½ tsp powder cinnamon
4 grated cloves
2 big pieces grated mastic

METHOD

1. Dissolve the yeast in two cups of warm water. Add the white flour and make a soft and sparse dough, place it on a warm floured surface, and cover with a cloth, so it rises.

2. In a big open bowl mix the olive oil, the orange juice, the raki, the sugar, the spices and combine well by hand.

3. Add the risen yeast to the mixture and knead one more time.

4. Add the barley flour gradually until well combined into a soft mixture.

5. Add water or flour if needed. Shape with hands into small rolls and place them on an oiled cooking tray.

6. Cover with a warm cloth to rise. Bake in the oven for 45-55 minutes at 180° C

Olives

THE MOST IMPORTANT FOOD

Grandmother was ninety eight years old and came from the highlands of Crete. She was one of those women that when you asked them about recipes they answered disarmingly " What recipes are you talking about ? We ate whatever we found in our gardens and in the countryside. And what do you think we treated people to back then? A handful of olives and some barley rusk, or two or three walnuts with raisins. Even in winter time when men went to the fields, they ate sauté olives and dipped a piece of bread into the wine. Olives are very nutritious and at those times we didn't have dummies for our babies so we sewed an olive inside a thin piece of cloth and we hung it around their necks."

*Traditional olive baskets
with their harvest*

THE NUTRICIOUS / FEEDING VALUE OF EDIBLE OLIVES

According to a very recent research which was conducted by the National School /Organization of Public Health (Food and Biochemistry branch),the general Chemical Laboratory of the Government and the Research Company and Technological Development Food Industry S.A. about the nutricious value of the Greek variety of olives, olives are sources of vegetative bran metals as well as monounsaturated fatty acids, which have beneficial reaction for health. The content of A tokopherole (vitamin E) in olives is remarkable, which affects as a natural antioxidant. A variety of Greek edible olives (Throumbes, black, green and the olives in the area of Kalamata) have been studied, which undergo the same preparation procedure (make them less bitter, by changing water and placing alternatively in salted water and vinegar) so big fluctuations don't occur as far as their food composition is concerned.

Olives in Greece, are an independent,

unique starter and a traditional product. On the contrary to their neighbouring societies, Greeks prefer to taste their original form, as a snack or a starter and inspite of their variety, rarely mixed in stews or pastries and various salads. In reality, olives are either green and less bitter, or black and slightly salted and wrinkled, or in a transparent mixture of vinegar, salt and oil, they form one of the most important appetizers or accompaniments to Greek meals. The annual average consumption of olives in Greece is three kilos per person. Greek consumers show a significant preference to the salty wrinkled olive as well as to the natural black olive, both of which are from family olive trees and prepared by the house wives themselves. In the older times, olives were an essential component of snacks, at least for the agricultural population, or for quick and easy meals in the evening, especially in Crete and Peloponissos where olives usually accompanied various hot drinks,

made from herbs, together with wheat and barley rusks. Even nowadays, barely any cold ouzo or raki reaches the Greek table not being accompanied by the classic snack: salted or vinegar olives on a plate with tomato, sardine and feta cheese. In the traditional Greek gastronomy, olives have always been accompanied by pulses, but also various fasting dishes with vegetables, like spring artichokes, fresh broad beans and different types of onions. Another ideal accompaniment to olives is the aromatic Greek summer tomatoes, a kind of salad herb (glistrida), feta cheese and onions.

RECIPES WITH OLIVES

1. OLIVE OIL PASTA WITH BLACK OLIVES

INGREDIENTS

1cup olive oil
500 gr /1lb pasta
1 large onion, sliced
250 gr /8 oz black olives, pitted
400 gr /13oz canned tomatoes, drained and roughly chopped
1 tbsp chopped parsley
salt and pepper
few sprigs of flat leaf parsley, to garnish

METHOD

1. Heat a large frying pan or wok and dry fry the onion for 3-6 minutes turning constantly, until soft. Add the olives and cook for 10 minutes.
2. Add the tomatoes the parsley, salt and pepper to taste. Bring to the boil, stirring. Cover the pan and simmer while cooking the pasta.
3. Meanwhile, bring a large saucepan of salted water to the boil. Add the pasta, stir and cook for 10-12 minutes until al dente. Drain well and place in a warm serving dish.
4. Add the sauce and toss lightly together. Garnish with the parsley and serve at once.

A vast selection of Greek olives at a big market in Athens

2. LAMB SWEET AND SOUR AND GREEN OLIVES

INGREDIENTS

1 kg, leg of a little lamb, cut in portions
1 crushed garlic clove
1 tbsp sugar
1 tsp honey
1 small crushed onion
1 cup vinegar of white wine
½ cup olive oil
1 cup green salted pitted olives
1 cup of soup (meat broth)
salt, freshly ground green pepper, rosemary, juice of 1 medium lemon

METHOD

1. Wash and dry the portions of the lamb. Season with the salt, the pepper, the garlic and the rosemary.
2. In a saucepan sauté the olive oil with the onion and the lamb, until golden.
3. Pour a cup of water and meat broth around the meat. Simmer covered for 45-50 minutes.
4. Add the vinegar, cook gently so the liquids evaporate, adding the fine sugar, the honey and the olives.
5. Stir with a spoon and add a little more sugar or vinegar according to taste.
6. Simmer for a further 10 min. Five minutes before cooking is completed, pour the lemon juice around.
7. Remove from the heat and let it stand for 10 minutes before serving with the olives and the sauce.

3. DUCK OR CHICKEN WITH GREEN OLIVES

INGREDIENTS

1 duck or a chicken about 1 ½ kg
25 green olives without kernel
10 black olives from Kalamata
2 tbsp olive oil
4 tbsp vermout
3 cups of chicken broth
salt, pepper

METHOD

1. Clean the duck and wash very well. Let strain and drain completely. Add salt and pepper to the duck externally and internally.
2. Leave the green olives in a bowl with warm water for an hour.

3. Heat the olive oil in a large deep, saucepan, add the duck cut in 2 or 4 pieces and sauté.

4. Drizzle with the vermout, add the chicken broth, cook at 150° C for 45-50 minutes, turn the pieces of meat once or twice, every 15 minutes.

5. Remove the duck from the saucepan, keep warm in a low temperature oven.

6. In the meantime, continue to boil the sauce at high temperature, 200ºC, for 4-5 minutes until thickened.

7. Add the olives and continue to boil for another 2 minutes. Serve the duck with the sauce and the olives.

4. BAKED RABBIT WITH GREEN OLIVES

INGREDIENTS

1 rabbit clean and cut in 8 or 10 portions
½ of cup olive oil
1 cup white wine
4 sprigs fresh rosemary
2 big onions, cut in medium pieces
5 garlic cloves clean and crushed with the flat surface of the knife
1 tbsp peel of lemon, finely chopped
1 cup of green olives
salt, pepper, juice of 2 medium lemons

METHOD

1. Wash the rabbit and drain the portions well.

2. Season every portion separately with salt and pepper and arrange all of them into a porringer.

3. Mix the olive oil with the wine, the rosemary, the onions the juice the garlic and the peel of the lemon.

4. Pour the marinade over the pieces of the rabbit leave to season for at least 12 hours.

5. Put the pieces of the rabbit in a deep baking dish or in

an oven proof dish, and pour around the marinade. Bake uncovered in preheated oven at 190°C for 15-18 min. and recover the meat often with its sauce.

6. Finally add the olives and bake low, at 150°C for about 1 hour and 20 minutes.

7. If it gets a gold brown colour, cover with aluminum foil. Serve hot with its sauce, without the rosemary.

5. SALAD WITH BEANS ALMONDS AND BLACK OLIVES

INGREDIENTS

½ kg fresh black eye beans
3 tbsp parsley finely chopped
2 tbsp peeled almonds finely chopped
1 cup black olives finely chopped
1 ½ cup mayonnaise
4 boiled eggs cut in round slices
salt

METHOD

1. Clean the beans, wash them and cut them in half or in three pieces if large.
2. Boil in plenty of salted water. Remove from the heat, strain and dry in a strainer. Set aside to cool.
3. Roast the almonds for a little and leave aside also to cool. In a deep serving salad bowl, arrange the beans and stir in the olives, the almonds and a pinch of salt. In another smaller bowl whisk the mayonnaise with the parsley, drizzle the dressing over the salad and garnish with the egg slices.

6. SALAD WITH OLIVES AND ORANGE

A very tasty salad, that combines the acidity of the orange fruit, the sweetness of the potatoes and the tempting spicy taste of the olives.

INGREDIENTS

6 medium size, boiled potatoes
1 orange cut in small pieces(without the peel)
1 big onion finely chopped
10 Kalamata olives
3 tbsp extra virgin olive oil
1 tsp vinegar
1 tsp oregano
salt, pepper

METHOD

1. Arrange the cold boiled potatoes and cut in to cubes, season with the salt, oregano and the pepper.

2. Drizzle lightly with the vinegar. Add the pieces of the orange, the onion, the olives and finally the olive oil.

3. Toss with two forks and serve the salad at room temperature.

4. This salad is an ideal accompaniment, to roasted pork, or to young turkey.

7. SALAD WITH BLACK AND GREEN OLIVES FINELY CHOPPED

INGREDIENTS

1 cup black olives, finely chopped
1 cup brine green olives, finely chopped
½ cup finely chopped olives
1 tsp sweet paprika
½ tsp chilli pepper
1 crushed garlic clove
2 tbsp parsley finely chopped
1 tbsp lemon juice
2 tbsp olive oil

METHOD

1. In a bowl add the olives, the parsley, the pepper, the paprika and the garlic.
2. Mix the mixture well until all the ingredients have been incorporated.
3. While stirring with a wooden ladle, add the lemon juice and the olive oil gradually. Season to taste. Stand for 20 minutes and serve with fresh toasted bread.

8. SALAD WITH COURGETTES, APPLE, OLIVES AND SAUCE OF HAZELNUTS

INGREDIENTS

4 medium size courgettes, cut in lengthwise pieces
1 red apple unpeeled, cut in small pieces
4 green olives finely chopped
For the dressing:
1 cup hazelnuts
2 garlic cloves crushed with a pinch of salt
2 tbsp strained bag yogurt
1 tbsp parsley finely chopped
juice of a medium lemon
salt, pepper

METHOD

1. Soak the courgettes in plenty of salted water for 10 minutes. Remove, strain and dry well on kitchen towel.
2. Cut the apple into thin oblong wedges and immerse them in boiling water for 4-5 minutes. Let them drain on kitchen paper.
3. Arrange the courgettes, the wedges of the apple in a large bowl, add the olives, season with salt and pepper and prepare the sauce as follows.
4. In an electric grinder pulp the hazelnuts with the salt

and the garlic, pour in the olive oil and the juice of lemon drop by drop and lastly the parsley.

5. Pour this sauce around the courgettes and the apple, sprinkle with a pinch of pepper and serve immediately.

9. PORRIDGE WITH OLIVES AND LENTILS

INGREDIENTS

1 cup of lentils
1 tbsp brandy
1 cup pitted black olives
1 tbsp caper
2 anchovies fillet
2 crushed garlic cloves
½ tsp sweet paprika dry red pepper
1 tsp oregano
small quantity of black pepper
3 tbsp lemon juice
4 tbsp extra fine olive oil
5 toast slices or pita bread

METHOD

1. Pick, wash and strain the lentils. Fill with warm water to cover the lentils. Boil for 20 minutes.
2. After the 20 min. add the cognac and if necessary water. Continue cooking for a further 10 minutes.
3. Strain the lentils and keep 1 cup of their broth aside. Soak the olives, the caper, the anchovies for 10 minutes in cold water. Let them dry on kitchen towel to absorb excess liquids and set aside.
4. Mix the crushed garlic with the broth from the lentils, the oregano, the paprika or the red pepper and the black pepper.
5. Empty the broth with the others ingredients in a small pot and boil at high temperature for 5 minutes.
6. Blend the olives, the caper, the anchovies, the lentils with the broth of the lentils, in a food processor in quick turns.
7. Drop the lemon juice and the olive oil in gradually. According to taste add a little lemon juice.
8. Transfer the porridge into a bowl, cover with kitchen foil and keep refrigerated for one hour, until the flavours of the ingredients combine well. Serve with toasted bread or pita bread.

10. OLIVES AND CAPER PASTE

INGREDIENTS

2 cups pitted black olives
1 tbsp caper
4 sardine fillets (without the bone)
1 garlic clove
5 tbsp olive oil

METHOD

1. Rinse the olives thorougly under cold running water for 4-5 minutes.

2. Wash the fillets of the sardines well and leave them on kitchen paper to strain. Strain the olives and blend with the fillets of the sardines, the caper and the garlic.
3. Turn at low speed and start to blend the mixture, add spoonfuls of the oil gradually.
4. Empty this olive paste the into a bowl, cover with and put in the fridge for 30 minutes, to incorporate all the flavours.

11. SALTY BREAD WITH GREEN OLIVES AND PAPRIKA

INGREDIENTS

500 gr all purpose flour
1 tsp salt
1 tsp fresh yeast
1 tbsp sweet paprika
1 tbsp olive oil
8 big green olives finely chopped
1 tbsp coarse salt

METHOD

1. Dissolve the yeast in one cup of warm water, add the olives and the salt. In a small frying pan heat the oil with the paprika.
2. Saute for 3-4 minutes until the aroma from the paprika evaporates.
3. Empty this mixture over the other ingredients, stir with the flour.
4. Knead the dough at maximum speed until well combined to a soft and elastic dough, (add water or flour if needed).
5. Place dough on floured surface and shape with hands into oval and flat bread and press the surface gently with the palm of your hand.
6. Cover with a cotton cloth and let it stand to rise for about 40 minutes.
7. Bake in preheated oven at 180º C, for 35-40 minutes, until golden on top.
8. With a moist finger press all over the surface and sprinkle the sea salt on top.

Green and purple olives marinated in lemon and bitter lemon juice

12. PIE WITH BASIL, TOMATO SAUCE, OLIVES AND CHEESE

INGREDIENTS
FOR THE DOUGH/ PASTRY

250 gr all purpose flour
2 tbsp olive oil
1 cup basil finely chopped
1 tsp salt
1 tsp pepper

Ingredients for the filling:
1 kg ripe tomatoes
2 eggs
10 round, black olives
½ tsp sugar
1 tsp salt
250 gr haloumi cheese or mozzarella, cut in thin, oblong pieces
3 tbsp olive oil
½ tsp pepper

DOUGH METHOD

1. In a large bowl prepare the dough mixing firstly the flour with the basil, the salt and the pepper.
2. Add the olive oil and a little warm water. Mix until well combined to a tight mixture.
3. Wrap the ball of dough in cling film and leave it outside the fridge for 20 min.
4. For the filling, dip the tomatoes for 2-3 minutes in hot water, peel, deseed and blend them.
5. Transfer the blended tomato in to a frying pan with the olive oil and simmer covered for 10 minutes, add the sugar, the salt and the pepper and continue to boil for a further 3-4 minutes. In the meantime break the eggs and mix quickly with the tomato sauce.
6. Finish off cooking with the temperature in the off position, transfer from the heat and let it cool for a little.
7. Arrange, the dough in a lightly oiled baking dish, scatter over some beans to prevent the dough from rising Bake at 180° C for 20 min.
8. Remove from the oven, subtract the beans and put the filling in. Spread in the filling on the top and arrange the pieces of cheese on top forming a lattice design.
9. Put the olives in the spaces and bake at 180° C for 25 min. Serve at room temperature, never warm.

13. SALTED GREEN OLIVES

This recipe is ideal for all types and sizes of green olives, even the smallest one.

INGREDIENTS

1 ½ kg fresh whole olives
1 cup coarse salt
1 lt water
½ cup of olive oil
2 big glass jars with tight fitting lids
1 cup gravel or a big stone, or something very heavy

METHOD

1. Clean and wash the olives well from the stems, and leaves, and throw away the crushed or marked olives.
2. If the olives are big and fleshy you can make a cut in them length wise. Drain the olives from their liquids and empty them into a deep glass bowl. Fill with cold water, to cover them well. For this reason, it is necessary to wash the gravel or the stone well- don't use anything metallic- and wrap it in with a thin cloth. It is used as a weight to stop the olives from emerging to the surface.
3. Change the water daily for 7-8 days, if the olives are big and cut or 10-11 days if they are whole. Always fill with clean cold water. The olives must be bitterish.
5. Empty the water and wash the olives well under cold runnig water. Put them into the jars and prepare the brine.
6. Heat the water and put the salt in it , stir well until the salt dissolves then let the salted water cool. The duration of time you want to conserve the olives, not only depends on the quantity of the salt, but also how salty you prefer the taste of the olives.
7. Empty the cold brine into the pots, where the olives are, leave only enough space, about one-two fingers, over there you will add olive oil, so that it doesnt become moldy. Cap the jars tightly and keep in a cool place for at least 8 weeks before consuming the olives.

14. EMERGING BLACK OLIVES

INGREDIENTS

3 kilo big, fleshly, black, ripe olives
4 cups salt
8 cups water
1 ½ cup olive oil
2 tsp oregano

METHOD

1. Heat half of the water and dissolve half of the salt in it.
2. Drop the olives into the cold salted water, place a heavy object on top of the olives to avoid emerging and leave them there without changing the mixture or the position of the pot.
3. After 40 days strain the olives, wash them well and prepare a new mixture with the rest of the salt and water.
4. In a sauce pan heat the olive oil gently and sprinkle the oregano on top. Stir well and remove from the heat. Let it cool completely.
5. Empty the olives into the clean salted water and leave them there for another 10 days.
6. Drain them from almost the whole quantity of brine and pour the olive oil and oregano on top of the olives.

They are conserved for up to 2 years without any particular alterations.

15. GREEN OLIVES WITH CARROTS, GARLIC AND CELERY

INGREDIENTS

1 kg green olives
2 garlic cloves finely chopped,
2 carrots finely sliced
1 cup of celery roughly cut
(steams and leaves)
2 cups of cauliflower florets.
1 lt white vinegar
½ cup olive oil
1 kg coarse salt

METHOD

1. Wash the olives well and leave them to strain and dry completely. Cut them on two sides lengthwise.
2. Place them in a jar which you have filled with cold water, change the water every day for 14 days. Make salted water and place the olives in it. Leave the olives there in a clay pot or plastic jar for 4-5 months.
3. In the meantime shake it 6-7 times. Pour out the salted water, put the carrots, the garlic the cauliflower florets and the celery in the jar. Fill to the top with vinegar and leave them there for 20-30 days before consuming.
4. Put some oil on the surface of the jar so the olives and vegetables don't come in contact with oxygen.

16. FRIED OLIVES WITH ONIONS AND THYME

INGREDIENTS

2 ½ cups olives (type throumbes)
1 large onion, cut in thin slices
1 tsp thyme
1 tsp oregano
1 ½ cup olive oil

METHOD

1. Soak the olives over night, or for at least 12 hours, in plenty of cold water. Rinse them with clean running water.
2. Strain the olives and place on kitchen towel, to absorb and dry completely. In a large, deep frying pan, heat the olive oil and sauté the onion until translucent.

3. Add the olives and fry them gently for 4-6 minutes. Empty the olives with their oil, on to a strainer and leave to strain well. Sprinkle the thyme and the oregano on top.
4. Shake the olives and serve slightly warm or cold. This recipe is an ideal method. Conserve the olives in the fridge.

17. FRIED OLIVES WITH TOMATO AND ROSEMARY

INGREDIENTS

2 cups olives (type throumbes)
½ tbsp tomato paste
1 tbsp rosemary
½ tsp freshly ground pepper
1 cup olive oil

METHOD

1. Soak the olives over night, or for at least 12 hours, in plenty of cold water.
2. Rinse them with clean running water.
3. Strain the olives and place on kitchen towel, to dry completely. In a large deep frying pan, heat the olive oil and sauté the olives for 4-5

minutes at a high temperature.
4. Dissolve the tomato paste in ½ cup of warm water and empty it in to the frying pan. Stir and sprinkle the rosemary and the pepper and simmer for another 3-4 minutes. Serve the fryied olives hot or slightly warm.